9-11:
The Giant Awakens

Jeremy D. Mayer

Georgetown University

THOMSON
WADSWORTH

Australia • Canada • Mexico • Singapore • Spain
United Kingdom • United States

To JC, WP, and AS.

Executive Editor, Political Science: David Tatom
Editorial Assistant: Dianna Long
Technology Project Manager: Melinda Newfarmer
Marketing Manager: Caroline Croley
Marketing Assistant: Mary Ho
Project Manager, Editorial Production: Emily Smith
Print/Media Buyer: Robert King
Permissions Editor: Elizabeth Zuber

Production Service: G&S Typesetters, Inc.
Photo Researcher: Terri Wright
Copy Editor: Bruce Owens
Cover Designer: Brian Salisbury
Cover Image: AP/Wide World Photos
Compositor: G&S Typesetters, Inc.
Text and Cover Printer: Webcom Limited

COPYRIGHT © 2003 Wadsworth, a division of Thomson Learning, Inc. Thomson Learning™ is a trademark used herein under license.

ALL RIGHTS RESERVED. No part of this work covered by the copyright hereon may be reproduced or used in any form or by any means— graphic, electronic, or mechanical, including but not limited to photocopying, recording, taping, Web distribution, information networks, or information storage and retrieval systems—without the written permission of the publisher.

Printed in Canada

1   2   3   4   5   6   7   06   05   04   03   02

For more information about our products,
contact us at:
Thomson Learning
Academic Resource Center
1-800-423-0563
For permission to use material from this text,
contact us by: **Phone:** 1-800-730-2214
Fax: 1-800-730-2215
Web: http://www.thomsonrights.com

Library of Congress Control Number:
2002105843
ISBN 0-534-61659-3

Wadsworth / Thomson Learning
10 Davis Drive
Belmont, CA 94002-3098
USA

Asia
Thomson Learning
5 Shenton Way #01-01
UIC Building
Singapore 068808

Australia
Nelson Thomson Learning
102 Dodds Street
South Melbourne, Victoria 3205
Australia

Canada
Nelson Thomson Learning
1120 Birchmount Road
Toronto, Ontario M1K 5G4
Canada

Europe / Middle East / Africa
Thomson Learning
High Holborn House
50/51 Bedford Row
London WC1R 4LR
United Kingdom

Latin America
Thomson Learning
Seneca, 53
Colonia Polanco
11560 Mexico D.F.
Mexico

Spain
Paraninfo Thomson Learning
Calle/Magallanes, 25
28015 Madrid, Spain

Contents

Acknowledgments

This book grew out of conversations with Clare Lynch and David Tatom of Wadsworth. Thanks also to Dianna Long and Gretchen Otto.

Clyde Wilcox read this text in draft form and gave substantial feedback. Thanks also to George Carey and Ben Webster, who read portions of the manuscript. Thanks as well to Sam Mujal Leon and Jacquie Jones.

Jessica Karpuk of Georgetown University worked as my research assistant, and her input and editing were invaluable.

I'd like to thank the students in my fall section of U.S. Political Systems at Georgetown University. Several students wrote research papers on the response of the government to the 9-11 crisis, which helped shaped my own thinking on these difficult questions. In particular, I'd like to thank: Maggie Daher, Julia Forrester, Jim Foster, Jessica Karpuk, Mark Largess, Brian McGovern, Dan Kim, Srirangar Dattatreya, Whitney Holmes, Lili Houseman, and Julia Baugher.

Jacqui Olkin was one of the first people I called on 9-11, and her love and support during the writing of this brief text were vital to its completion.

I dedicate this textbook to three friends who have been part of my life for decades. Hearing from Anne, Walt, and Jon in the hours and days after the towers were hit reassured me that while much had changed forever, some things never do.

This book was born out of a terrible tragedy, and I am mindful that for the families and friends of the victims and survivors, the attacks of 9-11 will never be matters for cold academic analysis. My modest goal in writing this text is to put a national tragedy into a political context, so that college undergraduates will have a better grasp of what happens when a democratic republic is attacked by the enemies of an open society.

A portion of my fee for the writing of this book has been donated to the Leslie Whittington and Family Memorial Fund. Dr. Whittington taught at the Georgetown Public Policy Institute, and was a passenger on American Airlines Flight 77 that crashed into the Pentagon. In memory of Leslie, her husband Charles Falkenberg, and her two daughters, Zoe, 8, and Dana, 3, who all perished on September 11th, Georgetown established this fund to support students and scholarship. To make a donation or to learn more about the fund, go to www.georgetown .edu/grad/gppi/whittington/memorialfund.html.

Jeremy D. Mayer
February 22, 2002
Washington, D.C.

INTRODUCTION

※

9-11:

The Giant Awakens

Those who expect to reap the blessings of freedom must, like men, undergo
the fatigues of supporting it. The event of yesterday was one of those kind
of alarms which is just sufficient to rouse us to duty, without being
of consequence enough to depress our fortitude.

THOMAS PAINE, *THE AMERICAN CRISIS,*
SEPTEMBER 12, 1777

On September 11, 2001, 19 international terrorists attacked the United States
of America by hijacking four airplanes and flying two of them into the World
Trade Center in New York City and one into the Pentagon in suburban Washington, D.C. Thousands died in New York as two of the world's tallest buildings crumbled while more than 100 died at the Pentagon, a symbol of America's
military might. The fourth hijacked plane was brought down in Pennsylvania by
the brave actions of the passengers on board, who perished saving the lives of perhaps thousands more in Washington, D.C., where the plane was heading. Between New York, Washington, Pennsylvania, the initial death toll estimates were
higher than the casualties suffered during any single day in the history of American warfare.

Shortly after 9:00 A.M., President George Walker Bush, on a tour of Florida,
was notified that the second plane had struck the World Trade Center. His chief
of staff, Andrew Card, whispered to Bush as the president spoke to a group of
elementary school students, "A second plane hit the second tower. America is
under attack." Bush, who had been stunned minutes before by the news of the
first plane crashing into the towers, was now faced with the most serious assault
against his country, certainly in his lifetime and possibly in the nation's existence.

The site of the World Trade Center smoldered for months following the terrorist attacks on 9-11. As late as April 2002, bodies were still being recovered from the rubble.

The moment was unprecedented in modern world history; the world's sole remaining superpower had been attacked not by another nation but by a shadowy band of outlaws owing allegiance to no country. So dominant had the United States been since the demise of the Soviet Union in 1991 that scholars of international relations had been fond of labeling the modern world a "unipolar system" in which the leadership of the United States was largely unchallenged. Perhaps as a consequence, the United States had been in retreat from the world, at least in terms of the public agenda, with foreign policy playing very little role in the presidential elections of 1992, 1996, and 2000. September 11 was a wakeup call, a message that the world could not be ignored, that superpower status has costs.

Filling the airwaves on September 11, even as the towers collapsed, were comparisons to another moment when the American public was jolted from an isolationist sleep: December 7, 1941, the morning when the Japanese launched a sneak attack on Pearl Harbor in Hawaii. The comparison was in many ways apt. America, while not a dominant power in 1941, was certainly an important nation that had retreated from world leadership following World War I. Its military forces were underfunded and unprepared. Many prominent Americans were loath to involve the nation in the troubles of Europe, content to watch France fall to the Nazis and to offer only tepid assistance as London was bombed nightly. December 7 was the turning point when America chose to engage with the problems of the world and eventually to rise to world leadership. On September 11, 2001, some Americans old enough to remember the emotions of December 7, 1941, even told reporters that the feelings and thoughts running through their minds were similar. A peaceful nation had suddenly found itself at war. A sleeping giant had been jolted awake by the sound of massive explosions and the screams of the dying.

While comparisons of Pearl Harbor and September 11 are natural, the differences are also crucial. The Japanese empire was a nation that had launched a sneak attack against the American military base at Pearl Harbor. Osama bin Laden's al-Qaeda terrorist network, while working closely with Afghanistan's Taliban government, had no permanent home. They had attacked civilians and had as their stated goal not the defeat of American forces but the killing of Americans. This time, the enemy had lived among us for years, hiding in our cities, attending our schools, and traveling repeatedly on the commercial jets they would turn into deadly missiles. The attacks of September 11 were as much a domestic challenge as a military one, raising troubling questions about how an open society could protect itself from suicidal opponents without respect for innocent life. While World War II also led to severe limitations on civil liberties, the domestic threat was far more apparent now.

Perhaps the most important difference was that the attacks took place at a time when America's political institutions were distinctly lacking in public support. Consider the most fundamental duty of citizens in a democratic republic: voting. Voter turnout in American elections has plummeted since the 1960 election; in 2000, even with the extraordinarily tight race between Al Gore and George W. Bush, barely half of Americans voted. In congressional and local elections, turnout is far lower. Ever since the tragedy of Vietnam and the scandal of Watergate, Americans have felt lower trust for their government.

There were also those who felt American society itself was weak. Many conservatives saw dangerous declines in important core values, such as honesty, patriotism, sexual fidelity, religious faith, and family integrity. Some liberals worried that Americans were becoming increasingly selfish and divided by class, with the wealthy cocooning themselves from the working classes in private neighborhoods and private schools. Political scientist Robert Putnam of Harvard University had argued for several years that Americans were experiencing declines in "social capital," or the level of voluntary activity in America's communities. Without such associations, Americans were becoming isolated. Assuming that there was at least some truth to these critiques of American society, we might have expected that the nation would not be willing to make the sacrifices that the "greatest generation" of 1941 did in response to Pearl Harbor.

The attacks of September 11 also threatened to alter the three key values that undergird our Constitution: separation of powers, individual liberties under limited government, and federalism. A national emergency naturally enhances the power of the president, who is, under the Constitution, the commander in chief of our armed forces and the chief executive of our federal departments. Indeed, the power to "make war" as opposed to "declare war" was explicitly denied to

What Is al-Qaeda? The Nature of the Enemy

Osama bin Laden appeared in several videotapes released to the media after 9-11. He and his followers did not deny their responsibility for the terrorist attacks on New York and Washington, D.C.

Although this book is about the domestic response of the U.S. political system to the attacks of September 11, it may be helpful to briefly outline the group that launched assaults on America.

Al-Qaeda (Arabic for "the base") is a terrorist organization founded by dissident Saudi and Egyptian radicals. These fanatical Muslims believe that God has called them to free the Arab and Muslim peoples of the world from what they perceive as American and Western physical oppression and cultural domination. The founder and leader of al-Qaeda, Osama bin Laden, is the son of a Saudi billionaire who played a minor role aiding the Mujahedeen fighters of Afghanistan in their struggle against the Soviet Union in the late 1980s. After returning to Saudi Arabia, bin

Congress because James Madison, the father of our Constitution, wanted the president to be able to "repel sudden attacks" on the nation. When the planes hit the Pentagon and the World Trade Center, the balance of power between the president and Congress changed, suspending the normal rules of American politics. At such times, the danger of executive abuse of power reaches its zenith; not only the American people must trust that their president is of high character, but so too must the members of Congress. They must trust that the president will not ex-

What Is al-Qaeda? The Nature of the Enemy (*continued*)

Laden was outraged when Saudi Arabia asked the United States to defend it against Iraq, which invaded Kuwait in 1990. The presence of so many Western troops near the holiest sites in Islam, the cities of Mecca and Medina, aroused bin Laden and his followers to fury. Expelled by his own country for his radical beliefs, bin Laden ended up back in Afghanistan. There, he founded al-Qaeda along with a radical group of Egyptian Muslims. Afghanistan's Taliban government, composed of hard-line Islamic radicals, welcomed al-Qaeda as a band of kindred spirits. Using his millions of dollars and his impassioned followers, bin Laden became an essential supporter of the Afghan government in its civil war with forces of the Northern Alliance, which had governed Afghanistan with extreme brutality from 1992 to 1996. In return for bin Laden's assistance, the Taliban granted him sanctuary in Afghanistan and allowed his group to run training camps for terrorist activities. Al-Qaeda was linked to a number of attacks on U.S. interests, most particularly the assault on U.S. embassies in Africa in 1998 and the attack in 2000 on the USS *Cole,* a Navy ship docked in Yemen.

Why has al-Qaeda conducted terrorist actions against the United States? They see the United States as propping up a number of corrupt Arab regimes, including Saudi Arabia and Egypt. The presence of U.S. troops in so many Muslim countries is a key complaint. The leaders of al-Qaeda also believe that American values such as gender equality, sexual freedom, individualism, and materialism threaten to erode the faith of Muslim people worldwide. Finally, many members of bin Laden's terrorist network are angered by America's support for the illegal Israeli occupation of Palestinian territories. While al-Qaeda's tactics are not supported by a majority of citizens in the Arab and Muslim world, many of their complaints are echoed by more mainstream groups in those countries.

Al-Qaeda and bin Laden had not escaped the notice of U.S. intelligence. For years, a team at the CIA headquarters in McLean, Virginia, had been devoted entirely to gathering information on his network of terror. The Clinton administration had authorized massive surveillance of bin Laden and had come close to killing him. Following the 1998 attacks on American embassies in Africa, President Clinton launched cruise missile strikes on bin Laden's camps in Afghanistan and on an alleged chemical weapons factory in Sudan (the Sudanese installation, which turned out to be a pharmaceutical factory, was entirely decimated). In the summer of 2001, the CIA even constructed an exact replica of bin Laden's villa and destroyed it with a Predator drone missile. The CIA finally had a way to eliminate bin Laden within minutes of locating him. Seven days before the attacks of September 11, members of Bush's cabinet considered for the first time a separate plan designed to force the Taliban to give up bin Laden or be removed from power. That these plans were under consideration in the Bush and Clinton administrations illustrates how seriously U.S. intelligence took the threat of al-Qaeda.

Of all the terrorist organizations across the world, al-Qaeda had established itself as the boldest, best trained, best financed, and most bloodthirsty. Thus, when it became clear to the president's national security team that an attack of unprecedented savagery and scope had taken place, the working assumption was that al-Qaeda was responsible. Evidence quickly emerge to confirm these suspicions.

ploit the situation, take only necessary steps, and return power to Congress when the crisis is passed. Similarly, the balance between liberty and order symbolized by our Bill of Rights comes under greatest strain during national crises. The judiciary has a history of construing government power much more broadly in a crisis than in peacetime. Prosecutors and police gain strength, and the rights of the accused come under severe assault. Finally, any national crisis centralizes our political system at the expense of state powers. Federalism, the delicate balance of power between state and national governments, cannot help but be changed by the attacks of September 11. For the past twenty years, Republicans and Democrats alike have collaborated to return more power to the states, but that trend may be halted by the attacks. Inevitably, tensions emerged between the federal and state governments. For example, the FBI demanded that local and state police agencies cooperate in the investigations of the attacks, but many localities complained that the FBI was not sharing information on suspects and tactics. In all these areas and many others, the attacks altered the way Americans thought about government and the way the government behaved toward its citizens.

Many pondered how the American political system would respond to the attacks of September 11. As the towers of the World Trade Center fell, it was an open question. The pages that follow attempt to provide an initial answer. We begin by examining the presidency, the focal point of American government in any crisis. We then take on the role that Congress played in the response to the attacks. Can 535 representatives of the people's will provide coherent national leadership in times of rapidly evolving danger? Should they make the attempt, or should they simply defer to the president? Next, we look at how the attacks of September 11 changed the nature of civil liberties in America and the judicial questions that emerged. Then we look at how the public mind has responded to the attacks. Will the effects be long lasting, or will the public mood return to the pre-attack equilibrium? Will this generation be forever changed by the experience of watching those towers fall, of knowing that there were forces in the world so full of hatred and so capable of violence that they would commit such an act? Finally, we briefly consider how the U.S. political system may continue to respond in the future as the ongoing crisis evolves. The U.S. political system underwent a terrible shock on September 11 that had constitutional, political, legal, and military ramifications. The story of the U.S. political system's response to the attacks is far from over. But the first six months since that catastrophic morning shed light on enduring truths about American politics and suggested areas where our society and our government may never be the same again.

1

✵

The President in Crisis: Challenge and Opportunity

It was a question no other president had been asked. Could President George W. Bush order the deaths of innocent Americans?

The World Trade Center and the Pentagon were burning. The Federal Aviation Administration had ordered all aircraft grounded, for the first time in U.S. history. Reports were reaching the president aboard *Air Force One* that not all planes could be accounted for. If another plane approached Washington or New York, should the hastily scrambled Air Force jets fire on it?

There was no legislation to guide Bush, no time to consult with the leaders of Congress, no precedent in U.S. history for Bush to follow. The Constitution provided only that the president would be the commander in chief. Alone with this awesome responsibility, Bush reluctantly gave the order that any commercial plane that refused orders to land should be blown out of the sky, regardless of the innocent passengers.

Fortunately, the order never had to be carried out. But that it was given at all illustrates how new was the world that George W. Bush, the 43rd president of the United States, found himself inhabiting following the terrorist attacks of September 11. Not since 1941 had American territory been attacked, and this time it was not an attack on a distant U.S. territory (Hawaii was not yet a state in 1941). This time, New York City, the economic capital of the nation and the world, and Washington, D.C., the seat of the national government, had been the victims of surprise assaults. Not since the British burned the White House during the War of 1812 had an enemy been so bold. And no enemy had made U.S. civilians the sole targets of violence.

As Bush flew from Florida, where he had been giving a speech on education as the planes hit the World Trade Center, the power of the president grew, as it always does in times of crisis. Bush was suddenly facing unique challenges and

Presidents in Crisis: Notable Moments in American History

The initial plan of the Founding Fathers was that the legislative branch would be the most important branch of government, exercising more will than the president and directing the president in many areas. One of the reasons that the system has evolved to its present state, in which presidents have much more power than was originally foreseen, is that presidents have accumulated power in various crises over time and failed to return all their new powers when the crises ended. The story of the growth of the presidency is in many ways a story of "growth in crises," foreign and domestic. Some memorable presidential responses to crises follow:

Abraham Lincoln: The Civil War

When rebellious Southern forces fired on Sumter, South Carolina, in 1860, Lincoln, newly inaugurated, blockaded Southern ports, suspended habeas corpus, increased the budget of the military, and instituted the draft. All these powers were constitutionally granted to Congress, but Lincoln took them without even consulting congressional leaders in order to save the Union.

Lincoln, in the view of many historians our greatest president, defended taking new powers unto himself during the Civil War: "Was it possible to lose the nation, and yet preserve the constitution? . . . measures, otherwise unconstitutional, might become lawful, by becoming indispensable to the preservation of the constitution, through the preservation of the nation." Subsequent presidents have used Lincoln's behavior as justification for their own actions during crises.

Woodrow Wilson: World War I

Wilson, outraged that German submarines were sinking U.S. vessels in the Atlantic Ocean during World War I, asked Congress to arm the merchant ships. Congress refused, fearing that such an action would lead to war with Germany. The public was very much divided about getting involved in World War I, and Congress responded to this mood. However, Wilson's young assistant secretary of the Navy, Franklin Delano Roosevelt, found obscure statutory authority for Wilson to arm the ships by executive order. Wilson did so, and conflict with the German navy increased, eventually leading to the war that Congress had sought to avoid. Historians, however, give Wilson credit for later consulting extensively with Congress, even as he took on massive new powers to enable the successful leadership of America's war effort.

Franklin Roosevelt: World War II

From 1939 to 1941, America was officially neutral in the conflict between Germany and Britain. However, the British were in such dire straits as the Germans won battle after battle that Roosevelt, acting on his authority as commander in chief, took emergency steps to aid Britain, without congressional support and against existing statutes. For example, he traded American military ships to Britain in exchange for British bases in the Atlantic and engaged German naval forces in the Atlantic prior to the declaration of war. Roosevelt also seized several military factories without congressional authorization. The assistance that Roosevelt gave to Britain during this period led Germany and Italy to declare war on the United States following the Japanese attack on Pearl Harbor, thus drawing the United States into the European war on the side of Britain, as Roosevelt had wished.

dangers, but he would have available to him methods and measures that would have been off limits on September 10. The normal rules of American government and American politics were suspended. But Bush was not in a world without rules. The conduct of the president in crisis follows an established pattern. It evolves over time as chief executives address wars, domestic unrest, and economic upheaval. With the new powers granted to Bush to deal with this sudden threat came immense danger. Nothing else that Bush did would be as significant to the success or failure of his presidency as how he responded to this moment. The other major institutions in American politics—Congress, the judiciary, the states, even the bureaucracy—would willingly cede certain powers to Bush, but these powers would come with massive expectations. The greatest presidents in American history were those who rose to tremendous challenges—George Washington, Franklin Roosevelt, and above all Abraham Lincoln. But presidents who failed to lead the nation through times of crisis had quickly lost the support of the American public. When the Tet Offensive revealed in 1968 that Lyndon Johnson's Vietnam policy was failing, he found himself losing all credibility with the public. When Jimmy Carter failed to free the U.S. hostages from Iran in 1980, he was removed from office by a deeply disappointed American electorate. If Bush succeeded, his place in presidential history would be assured; if he failed, neither the public nor future historians would have mercy.

PRESIDENTS AND CRISES IN A THEORETICAL CONTEXT

The Constitution does not explicitly provide for a "state of emergency" as do many of the world's constitutions. In many countries, leaders have used such states of emergency to become tyrants and dictators by failing to declare an end to them. In America, crises do upset the normal distribution of power under the Constitution, certainly at least in part exactly as the founders intended. The authors of the Constitution were aware that in rapidly evolving crises, it might be impossible for Congress to convene or to come to speedy agreement. The necessity for a "single hand" to guide the government at certain times was one of Alexander Hamilton's best arguments for a strong executive. In a crisis, the president's power grows because of three factors: the constitutional grants of power, the deference of other branches, and the enhanced attention and support of the public.

The Constitution, Article II, Section 2, explicitly gives specific powers to the president in foreign and military matters:

> The president shall be commander in chief of the Army and Navy, of the militia of the several states, when called into the actual service of the United States. . . .
> He shall have power, by and with the advice and consent of the Senate, to make treaties, provided two thirds of the Senators present concur, and he shall nominate, and by and with the advice and consent of the Senate, shall appoint ambassadors. . .
> . . . he shall receive ambassadors and other public ministers.

These powers are in addition to his role as chief executive. As the head of the national government, the president commands the loyalty of the secretary of state and all national security policymakers. They are constitutionally mandated to provide him with reports on their activities, and they serve at his pleasure. Finally, the president is also granted the power to "on extraordinary occasions, convene both

Houses, or either of them," implying that the Constitution foresaw a need for Congress to be hastily brought together in emergencies.

Of these crisis powers, none is more vital or more clearly granted than the president's position as leader of the military. As commander in chief, the president leads the largest military force in the Western world, with 1.4 million members under arms supported by 700,000 civilian employees. The military budget of the United States is larger than the next 15 nations combined. With the end of the Soviet Union, no other nation can match the technological prowess or force projection capabilities of the United States. Although Congress sets the budgetary guidelines of the military, the president's constitutional role as commander in chief is perhaps the most broadly construed and least challenged.

The deference extended by the other branches to the president during crises results from the explicit constitutional grants of power to the president. But the deference has grown over time, even without changes in the words of the Constitution. The willingness of Congress and the judiciary to defer to the president in crises has grown because of the changing nature of war and conflict. The speed with which international events occur forces Congress to allow presidents greater freedom today. The vast growth in America's overseas commitments has similarly altered the balance of power between the executive and Congress, as have the inventions of nuclear weapons and the intercontinental ballistic missile.

Consider the changes that developed in the 61 years from 1941 to 2002. Prior to World War II, the United States was not part of any large military alliances. In 1941, a president had the power to unilaterally respond to an attack on the United States, as Lincoln had in 1860, but attacks on few other nations would have justified an immediate response of the U.S. military without a congressional declaration of war. Today, America is responsible for the defense of dozens of countries, by treaties and executive orders. If South Korea, Japan, Britain, Germany, Canada, Australia, or a number of other nations were to come under serious and sudden attack, a president could bring U.S. forces into action without congressional permission. In 1941, U.S. troops were stationed in the United States and its territories almost exclusively. Today, we have troops under the president's command in dozens of nations around the world. Should those troops be fired on, no Congress would question the president's power to order an immediate and broad military response. These international commitments and military deployments are part of what historians call "the rise of the national-security state," which has fundamentally altered the balance of power between presidents and Congress. Vast as the president's power was from 1789 to 1948, it has been expanded by the deference shown to him by Congress as a result of historical shifts in war and conflict. Crises that involve the military and foreign policy in particular enhance the deference shown to the president. As political scientist Aaron Wildavsky argued, it may be useful to think of "two presidencies," one domestic, the other foreign. The domestic president faces challenges for control from Congress, the judiciary, interest groups, and the American public generally because those power centers are far more interested in domestic political issues than in foreign. In foreign policy, the constitutional powers of the president and the traditions of American politics give the executive greater autonomy with which to shape policies. The deference of Congress to the president in foreign policy is all the greater in a time of national crisis.

The president's power in crisis also grows because of the response of the American public. Since Teddy Roosevelt made the "bully pulpit" a part of the presidency, the public role of the office has expanded. Roosevelt exploited his position as the sole voice of the nation to gain power over Congress and to guide national policy. The emerging national mass media aided his efforts. Today, presidents explicitly seek to "go public," in the words of political scientist Samuel Kernell, to speak over the heads of Congress and the Washington establishment to the voters back home, an effort greatly aided by television. Recent work by presidential expert George Edwards suggests that many Americans are no longer watching presidents when they make speeches on important issues. Although this phenomenon lessens the impact of going public, in a crisis, the president has the nation's attention. The public rallies to him almost instinctively as a living symbol of the nation. For all these reasons, Bush could expect that the raw power available to him would be of a greater magnitude than that at the disposal of any president since F.D.R. What would Bush do with his vastly expanded powers?

THE BUSH ACTIONS: IMMEDIATE RESPONSES, INITIAL SETBACKS

The first steps that Bush took were to authorize air patrols over New York and Washington, to move our military to a heightened state of alert, to call up 35,000 military reservists to active duty status, and to focus our vast international intelligence network on the al-Qaeda organization. These steps and similar ones that Bush took to ensure the security of our borders were met with near unanimous support from Congress, the media, and the public. However, Bush faced more controversy with his personal actions in the hours and days after the attacks.

The president in modern times has been expected to be the "voice of the people," to speak for and to the nation in times of tragedy and danger. From the fireside chats of Roosevelt in the depths of the Depression to the powerful speech by John F. Kennedy during the Cuban missile crisis, the public has looked to the president to reassure the nation of his leadership and to explain the nature of the challenge facing the country. However, in his first comments from the site of his speech in Florida, Bush appeared shaky and did not effectively comfort the nation. He referred to the perpetrators as the "folks who committed this act" and promised that after his remarks he would return to Washington.

However, from Florida, Bush was flown to Louisiana, where he made another brief and ineffective statement of only 219 words, some of them mispronounced. He then flew again, not to Washington but to a military base in Nebraska. The Secret Service advised the president not to return to the White House until they could verify that no further terrorist assaults were planned. The Secret Service had reasons to be cautious: Earlier in the day, the White House had been fully evacuated by the Secret Service because the plane that had hit the Pentagon had

Presidential Rhetoric in Crises: A Comparison of Roosevelt and Bush

President George Bush raised the badge of police officer George Howard at the end of his September 20 speech, using it as a symbol of his commitment to fighting the war on terror.

One of the most famous speeches ever given by an American president was Franklin Delano Roosevelt's December 8, 1941, address to Congress. Among the many burdens placed on President Bush in the aftermath of September 11 was the need to measure up to the standard set by Roosevelt's war oration. Bush's September 20 speech to Congress was written by Michael Gerson, with the help of Karen Hughes and input from many other staffers. The president was involved at each step of the process, rejecting drafts and making suggestions. The two speeches are quite different. First, Bush's speech was nearly six times the length of Roosevelt's (3,023 words versus 515). The length and complexity of Bush's speech may reflect that he had nine days in which to prepare, whereas Roosevelt spoke to Congress as soon as it could be gathered.

These two historic speeches provide interesting contrasts. Roosevelt chose to open with blunt simplicity:

Yesterday, December 7, 1941—a date which will live in infamy—the United States of America was sud-

denly and deliberately attacked by naval and air forces of the Empire of Japan.

Bush, however, opened with a more indirect approach. Only in his tenth sentence did Bush begin to express the nation's anger:

Tonight we are a country awakened to danger and called to defend freedom. Our grief has turned to anger, and our anger to resolution. Whether we bring our enemies to justice, or bring justice to our enemies, justice will be done.

In his brief remarks, Roosevelt several times mentioned the nature of the Japanese sneak attack, reminding Americans that up until the very minute of the attack, Japanese diplomats were engaged in negotiations with U.S. authorities. In so doing, he rallied the country's anger:

Always will we remember the character of the onslaught against us. No matter how long it may take us to overcome this premeditated invasion, the American people in their righteous might will win through to absolute victory.

Presidential Rhetoric in Crises: A Comparison of Roosevelt and Bush

Bush also emphasized the malicious character of the assault on the country but spent at least as much time on the beliefs of America's new opponents, which Roosevelt largely ignored:

> *Al-Qaeda is to terror what the Mafia is to crime. But its goal is not making money; its goal is remaking the world—and imposing its radical beliefs on people everywhere. The terrorists practice a fringe form of Islamic extremism . . . a fringe movement that perverts the peaceful teachings of Islam. The terrorists' directive commands them to kill Christians and Jews, to kill all Americans, and make no distinction among military and civilians, including women and children.*

Roosevelt's speech was impersonal compared to Bush's. He did not, for example, mention Emperor Hirohito or any Japanese politicians or military leaders. By contrast, Bush mentioned Osama bin Laden by name, personalizing the enemy in America's new war. He also introduced to the nation and to Congress the widow of a murdered passenger and ended his speech by holding up the badge of a police officer lost in the rubble of the World Trade Center. Presidential speeches since Reagan have often included "real Americans" to illustrate the president's points and to tug at the heartstrings of the public. This approach would have struck many Americans as maudlin in 1941, but today it is expected and praised.

Bush included many other nations in his address, using his speech to continue the work of building an international coalition against terror. He even invited the prime minister of America's most faithful ally, Great Britain, to attend the speech so that he could thank the British personally for their support. Roosevelt, by contrast, did not mention that Japan had also attacked Great Britain, perhaps because the attack on Pearl Harbor had already made a coalition against fascism inevitable.

Bush used his speech to announce a new American policy, now known as the Bush Doctrine:

> *Every nation, in every region, now has a decision to make. Either you are with us, or you are with the terrorists. From this day forward, any nation that continues to harbor or support terrorism will be regarded by the United States as a hostile regime.*

One of the most important differences was that Bush included in his speech a call on Americans not to take out their anger on Muslim or Arab citizens:

> *We are in a fight for our principles and our first responsibility is to live by them. No one should be singled out for unfair treatment or unkind words because of their ethnic background or religious faith.*

Roosevelt, however, did not warn Americans against mistreating citizens of Japanese descent. Quickly, many Japanese Americans suffered from acts of violent revenge. Japanese businesses were attacked, and many Japanese either lost all their possessions or were forced to sell their belongings at fire-sale prices.

Roosevelt ended his address to Congress by predicting victory and calling on God for assistance:

> *There is no blinking at the fact that our people, our territory and our interests are in grave danger. With confidence in our armed forces, with the unbounding determination of our people, we will gain the inevitable triumph. So help us God.*

Bush's speech ended similarly:

> *The course of this conflict is not known, yet its outcome is certain. Freedom and fear, justice and cruelty, have always been at war, and we know that God is not neutral between them. Fellow citizens, we'll meet violence with patient justice—assured of the rightness of our cause, and confident in the victories to come. In all that lies before us, may God grant us wisdom, and may He watch over the United States of America.*

It is too early to tell whether Bush's speech to the nation on September 20 will achieve the legendary status of Roosevelt's December 8 address. The key may well be whether journalists and the public identify a single phrase or sentence from Bush's speech as capturing the mood of the nation. Roosevelt's "a day that will live in infamy" has become one of the most famous phrases in presidential rhetoric, while much of the rest of his speech is forgotten. (Roosevelt inserted the word "infamy" at the last minute in place of the far blander "world history.") The phrase captured the sense of outrage Americans felt at the sneaky nature of the Japanese attack. The most likely phrases to endure for the ages from Bush's speech are the one about bringing al-Qaeda to justice or bringing justice to them or the outline of the Bush Doctrine quoted here.

appeared to have been headed for the White House first. Vice President Dick Cheney gave the same advice, also mentioning that there was a vague new threat to *Air Force One*. Reluctantly, Bush agreed to wait, and made initial decisions while secluded in a bunker in Nebraska. When the president finally arrived at the White House that night, muted criticism of the president was already emerging. Had he shown the necessary courage in his personal conduct? Had this president, who had avoided military service in Vietnam, demonstrated cowardice? What message did it send to America, or at least to the residents of New York and Washington, that their president had not felt safe enough to return to the nation's capital and instead had holed up at a secure bunker in Nebraska? When it was later revealed that there had been no specific threat to *Air Force One* and that Cheney's warning was a product of miscommunication, criticism deepened. The subtext of the questioning of Bush's behavior on September 11 was obvious: Did Bush have the stature, the intellect, the character, and the eloquence to lead the nation in the first great challenge of the century?

Many observers remained unsure about whether he had those qualities following his address to the nation from the White House on the evening of September 11. Similarly, when Bush arranged for news cameras to witness a phone call with Mayor Rudy Giuliani and Governor George Pataki of New York, his attempts to convey his sympathy and resolve did not seem at all presidential to some. *Time* magazine correspondent Margaret Carlson wrote that Bush "looked like a teenager making weekend plans"—hardly an uplifting description. Moreover, Bush seemed to shrink in comparison with Mayor Giuliani, who was winning universal praise for his calm, informed, resolute tone and righteous anger, which many compared to the brave demeanor of Winston Churchill during the dark days of Britain's struggle with Nazi Germany. In the modern media age, a vital part of the president's job is to rally the nation, and it seemed that Bush was barely sufficient to the task.

In his visit to Ground Zero, the smoking wreckage that had once been the World Trade Center, Bush seemed to find his voice in talking to the rescue workers. In his impromptu speech to them and in his address at a national prayer service at the National Cathedral in Washington, he began to rise to the moment, to comfort a nation reeling from a sudden and unprecedented attack. However, expectations rose for his coming speech to Congress, at which he would be compared to the great presidents of the past. Would he be able to explain the events of September 11, his actions in response, and his plans for the future? Would he rally the country to his agenda for a post–September 11 world?

By the time Bush spoke to Congress on September 20, the stakes were as high as they had been for any presidential address since 1941. Not only had the initial assaults rocked Americans' complacency and sense of security, but the economy seemed to be in a free fall. The airlines, which had already been weak, were hurt by the lengthy grounding of commercial airline flights and laid off 80,000 workers because of expectations of recession and the fear of traveling. The New York Stock Exchange, located not far from the World Trade Center, reopened days after the attack but immediately lost $1.4 trillion in share values as stocks fell faster than they had since the Depression. Consumer confidence in the economy dropped, and economic hard times loomed. Bush would also have to address the question of domestic security; many Americans feared further terrorist attacks and wanted their government to take radical new steps to prevent them.

Bush's speech before Congress, which lasted for nearly an hour, was met with nearly universal approval. In it, he emphasized how America was facing a new and unique challenge, but he referred back to the unchanging and resilient character of the nation. His simple but ringing rhetoric struck a chord with the American public, according to polls. Citizens responded to his measured anger and the promise of swift action. Bush gave an ultimatum to the Taliban government of Afghanistan: If they did not turn over the terrorists, they would face severe consequences. He announced what has become known as the "Bush Doctrine": America will make no distinction between terrorists and a nation harboring them. Bush also announced the appointment of his personal friend, Pennsylvania Governor Tom Ridge, to head the new Office of Homeland Security.

In the view of most Americans, Bush had overcome his early miscues and found his mission and his moment, successfully fulfilling a central role of the modern president: rallying the nation in crisis. However, the challenges ahead would not be solved by rhetoric, however well crafted or delivered.

BUSH VERSUS THE BUREAUCRACY: CONFLICT IN CRISIS

September 9, 2001: On a Maryland highway, state trooper Joseph Catalano makes a routine speeding stop. He checks the Virginia driver's license of the driver, Ziad Samir Jarrah, and gives him a $270 ticket for driving 25 miles an hour over the speed limit. Two days later, Jarrah would become infamous as the likely pilot of the hijacked plane that crashed in Pennsylvania. A Maryland politician would later complain that the FBI had not provided enough information on the suspected terrorists and that better communication between federal authorities and state police might have stopped the hijacking. Other politicians complained of a lack of coordination between the Immigration and Naturalization Service (INS) and local police. If Jarrah, for example, had been one of the hijackers on an expired visa, it is unlikely that the traffic cop would have known this. There is so little coordination between the INS and states that driver's licenses remain valid after visas expire. Whether better cooperation between federal and state agencies would have prevented the terrorist attacks of September 11 is a question that cannot be answered. It is clear, however, that the multitude of federal, state, and local agencies that administer the fight against terrorism, from the cop on the beat to the White House anti-terror office, are often inefficiently deployed and unable even to communicate with each other, let alone coordinate their response. Our federal agencies cannot even agree on what terrorism is.

Why are bureaucracies unable to agree on a definition of terrorism and join together in the fight against it? It is not that the men and women who work at these agencies are unwilling. The reasons for the failure of federal and state agencies to effectively coordinate their efforts have to do with a multitude of "bureaucratic pathologies"—problems inherent in large hierarchical organizations with divergent agendas and mandates.

In his speech to the nation, Bush announced the creation by executive order of the Office of Homeland Security, with cabinet-level status for its leader, Tom Ridge. Bush hoped that Ridge would bring order and efficiency to the government's domestic response to terror. Almost immediately, the appointment came under attack from Democrats and some Republicans. The criticism had nothing to do with the choice of Ridge but rather with the way in which the office had been established. Ridge was intended to be the "terrorism czar" to cut through the red tape and bureaucratic hurdles that prevent effective terrorism prevention. Currently, more than four dozen federal agencies share some responsibility for fighting terror.

Ridge was charged with coordinating the activities of these agencies and providing advice to the president on how the terrorism battle should be managed. The idea of appointing someone close to the president to guide the bureaucracy in a specific policy area was not new. Such an appointee is expected to harness the prestige and power of the president to force departments to make compromises and combat various bureaucratic tendencies that block good public policy. A president does not have the time to follow the implementation of his policies throughout various bureaucracies or to monitor turf battles in the maze of Washington power. But no single cabinet secretary can claim to speak without bias or to speak with the president's authority in all cases. A "czar," located in the White House, is theoretically able to do both while focusing national attention on the administration's efforts in a policy area. Unfortunately, the history of such White House coordinators left many in Congress worried. For example, various presidents had tried to appoint drug czars and AIDS czars in the past, with limited success. Indeed, Clinton had already appointed a White House coordinator for terrorism, although unlike Ridge he did not enjoy cabinet-level status. Bureaucratic pathologies, such as turf protection, or the desire to maintain control over a certain issue or policy, defeated many such efforts in the past. Federal departments are highly reluctant to give up core functions in the name of efficiency. Congressional leaders feared that Ridge, without a substantial budget, firing authority over any of the anti-terror agencies, or a large staff, would not have the clout to manage homeland security.

In the midst of the debate over Ridge's appointment, the nation suffered another terrorist attack: mail-borne anthrax. Media outlets in New York and Florida and congressional offices in Washington were sent envelopes containing anthrax spores. Several infected citizens died, and more were hospitalized. Thousands of Americans were placed on harsh antibiotics as a preventive measure, and public concern reached a fever pitch. Ridge, facing a new threat in his first days on the job, did not appear to be informed or even involved in the key decisions. Critics in the media questioned whether the Office of Homeland Security was coordinating the nation's response or merely adding another layer of bureaucracy to an already confused situation. The media expectations on Ridge may have been unfair (the man was expected to have mastered the complexities of the weaponizing of anthrax spores in a few hours), but they reflected the public's desire for an effective and immediate response to the new threat. Ultimately, Ridge's staff is expected to grow to over 100, divided into 11 areas, but this will still be miniscule in comparison with the dozens of other agencies holding responsibilities for various portions of the battle against terrorism. It remains unclear whether the nation is any safer since the appointment of a terrorism czar.

Most Americans following Bush's speech on September 20 might have imagined that the greatest challenge facing the nation was to defeat the Taliban and capture al-Qaeda. But the bureaucratic challenges facing Bush and Ridge may be at least as difficult. Consider what must be done within the Justice Department alone, one of the key agencies in the fight against terror. Attorney General John Ashcroft has to cut 10 percent of his headquarters staff; reallocate those staff positions around the country as additional agents, prosecutors, and analysts; and put an additional 10 percent of his budget toward anti-terrorism. In the next fiscal year, the Justice Department will be hiring new staff and allocating new money provided by Congress to further fight terrorism. The FBI, a quasi-independent agency under the Justice Department, is moving agents from drug enforcement to anti-terror work. Each of these moves means hastily reorganizing departments, retraining and relocating staff, and reallocating money. Bureaucracies almost instinctively resist such disruptive measures.

Or consider the difficulties facing the INS. Reformers inside and outside Congress have called for changes in this much-criticized agency for years, yet the bureaucracy has remained impervious to such efforts. The attacks of September 11 focused the attention of Congress and the White House once again on the agency's failings. Thirteen of the 19 terrorists entered this country on legal visas, and some overstayed their limits. Terrorist ringleader Mohammed Atta was stopped at Miami International Airport by the INS for illegally trying to use a visitor's visa to attend flight school. However, when they learned that his student visa was being processed, they admitted him, a decision that was later subjected to intense criticism. But criticizing the INS for failing to stop the attacks may be asking too much of an already overworked agency. There are an estimated six million illegal aliens tracked by just 2,000 INS agents. The INS is partially responsible for monitoring the 4,000-mile border with Canada, but funding is so low that some of the checkpoints are not even manned and rely on the honor system. Given the multitude of tasks and the paucity of funding, it is not surprising that when the CIA put out a warning on two of the terrorists who would go on to attack New York, the INS was unable to locate them. There is no evidence that they even tried. The INS is underfunded for the tasks it is assigned, and those tasks are often in deep conflict. In the view of one former INS administrator, the agency "has essentially evolved into a welcoming agency. . . . We treat the people who come to our doorstep as customers and look for some way to let them in." For years, many in Congress have suggested that the INS should be split into two agencies, one that naturalizes and one that controls visas and border security. Months after the attacks again revealed the systematic nature of the INS problems, no concrete progress has been made, although Ridge and Congress are still studying the question.

The attacks of September 11 present the Bush administration with the oppor-tunity to utilize congressional deference and public support to restructure aspects of the federal bureaucracy. But restructuring and refocusing bureaucracies is rarely easy and never simple.

THE MILITARY RESPONSE:
BUSH AS WAR LEADER

"We will not waver, we will not tire, we will not falter, and we will not fail." With these starkly simple words of resolve, President Bush, on October 7, launched Op-eration Enduring Freedom. Shortly before the presidential address, the military assault on Afghanistan began with the firing of Tomahawk cruise missiles from American and British ships in the Arabian Sea. The Taliban government had re-jected Bush's ultimatum of September 20, and the president wasted little time in bringing the full weight of America's vast military might on the comparatively tiny forces of Afghanistan. Bush, along with Secretary of State Colin Powell, had put together an international coalition in support of the attacks, much as his father had done in the months leading up to the Persian Gulf War. Bush the younger, who had less foreign policy experience than almost any chief executive in the last 50 years when he was inaugurated, had ably gathered America's allies and even ral-lied the partial support of some traditional American opponents, such as China, Russia, and Iran. Now the time had come to act. The 10th U.S. president to lead his nation into a major war, Bush had the nearly united support of the U.S. pub-lic and Congress on his side as he ordered the bombing of Afghanistan.

The move had long been expected. Indeed, Bush had explored military op-tions almost from the moment it became clear that bin Laden was responsible for the attacks. Bush had gone to Congress for approval of the use of force and received a nearly unanimous vote of confidence. Yet this was a luxury that Bush could indulge because of the nature of the crisis. Had Bush ordered immediate air strikes against Afghanistan in retaliation for September 11, as he had contem-plated, it is unlikely that Congress would have objected. As President Truman said after he ordered forces into Korea without a declaration of war, "The con-gressional power to declare war has fallen into abeyance because wars are no longer declared in advance." Since Truman's time, Congress has, in response to the abuse of presidential powers by Johnson and Nixon in Vietnam, passed the War Powers Act.

This act, which set time limits on the president's use of force without Con-gress's approval, has failed to return much authority for matters of war and peace to Congress. Indeed, since the War Powers Act was passed over President Ford's veto, every president has legally contested its constitutionality while abiding by its requirements in most cases. Bush, for example, notified congressional leaders in early September when he sent clandestine forces into Afghanistan to aid the Northern Alliance, the domestic opposition to the Taliban.

What Does the War Powers Act Require?

The War Powers Act (WPA) attempts to prevent presidents from getting the country into war without congressional approval. By the 1970s, with America's foreign commitments vastly expanded by the need to fight the Cold War, U.S. troops were present in so many danger spots that a president could start a war very easily. Once the bullets were flying and American troops were dying, it would be nearly impossible for Congress to oppose the war, as Congress had discovered to its regret in the Vietnam conflict. President Johnson had used a murky minor engagement with North Vietnamese forces to get Congress to broadly approve the use of force throughout Vietnam. Many members of Congress ended up feeling that the president had manipulated his powers as leader of the military to dupe Congress and the nation into an unwise war. The possibility that presidents might use their power as commander in chief to initiate wars was much on the mind of the framers of our Constitution. Many of them believed that one of the prime advantages of republican government over monarchy was that kings and emperors tended to get their nations into wars to boost their popularity and weaken domestic opponents. Even as written, the Constitution's grant of the power to command the military solely to the president was challenged by some delegates to the convention. A delegate from Connecticut worried that a president might "commence war" without Congress's approval despite the republican limits on presidential power. Congress in 1973 attempted to return the power to choose war to Congress.

The WPA required that presidents report to Congress whenever military deployments endanger American lives. Should Congress fail to approve of these deployments within 60 days, the president is given a further 30 days during which he must remove the troops from harm's way. The WPA has arguably limited presidents' ability to cavalierly engage in military deployments, such as President Johnson's sending of U.S. troops into the Dominican Republic in 1965. In somewhat similar circumstances 30 years later, President Clinton was far more hesitant to send U.S. forces into Haiti. However, it is difficult to say whether Clinton's reluctance had to do with the fear of public opposition or the fear that Congress would not authorize his actions under the WPA. Another factor limiting the effectiveness of the WPA is the speed with which modern wars are conducted. The 90-day limit on deployments would have allowed President Bush to complete his entire campaign against the Taliban. Finally, the WPA may in the end have done little more than codify Congress's deference to the executive in military matters. If a president orders U.S. forces into a war and the war goes well, Congress would be unlikely to object. If the war goes badly, the public will rally around the president and the flag, and any congressional critics risk looking as if they are siding with the killers of Americans.

Another legacy of the Vietnam era is the so-called Vietnam syndrome in American public opinion. Since the end of that war, the American public has tended to oppose military conflicts that involve U.S. casualties, unless direct national interests are involved. This has been seen as a limitation on U.S. presidents, who have been very reluctant to order U.S. forces into harm's way. In 1983, when President Reagan sent U.S. troops into Beirut, Lebanon, to help bring about peace between Israel, Lebanon, and the Palestinians, 241 Marines were killed by a suicide bomber in a single attack. Very shortly, all U.S. forces were redeployed offshore, away from harm. Many felt that Reagan was unwilling to argue to the American public that national interests were at stake in the Lebanon conflict. Similarly, in 1993, when 19 Americans died after U.S. troops in Somalia came under fire, President Clinton quickly withdrew the troops. The legacy of Vietnam

The Doomsayers and the War in Afghanistan: Does the Media Have a Negative Bias?

Political scientists have debated the nature of media coverage of politics for years. In addition to exploring whether the media is liberal or conservative, much attention has been focused on whether the media is simply giving Americans a negative impression of politics through relentlessly negative coverage of politicians and political events. "If it bleeds, it leads" is one easy characterization of the idea that the media loves to give bad news. Some have identified the media's penchant for negative news about politics as a cause of the lower levels of trust Americans have in their government. Defenders of the media suggest that it is merely fulfilling a critical function required in a democracy. If more journalists had aggressively challenged government actions in Vietnam or in the early stages of Watergate, perhaps these national tragedies need not have taken such a toll on the public's attitudes toward government. Blaming the media for declines in trust in government after the misdeeds of Watergate and Vietnam is truly a case of blaming the messenger in this view.

Still, unlike the U.S. public, which had a great deal of patience with President Bush's conduct of the war, many voices in the media were quick to label the war a failure. Consider these media quotes, collected by the *Wall Street Journal* after the war was successfully ended.

> "The United States is not headed into a quagmire; it's already in one."
> JACOB HEILBRUN, STAFF EDITORIAL WRITER, *LOS ANGELES TIMES*, NOVEMBER 4, 2001

> "This is a war in trouble."
> DANIEL SCHORR, *NATIONAL PUBLIC RADIO* COMMENTATOR, OCTOBER 27, 2001

> "We are mapless, we are lost, and we are distracted by gusts of wishful thinking."
> NICHOLAS VON HOFFMAN, *NEW YORK OBSERVER*, NOVEMBER 19, 2001

Although these are only three voices selected from the uncounted mass of columnists, pundits, and journalists who make up the American media, they were not alone. An unnamed expert in *Newsweek* cautioned in October that "the West shouldn't underestimate . . . the ferocity of the Afghans." Preeminent historian Arthur Schlesinger Jr. warned that the military had not learned the lesson of Vietnam and doubted that the Bush air strategy would work. The *New York Times,* perhaps the most influential newspaper in America, opined on October 31 that "signs of progress are sparse," and the war seemed to be going badly. Numerous media figures ridiculed the idea that the Northern Alliance would be able to defeat the Taliban without large assistance from U.S. ground troops. A few weeks later, the Taliban was almost entirely defeated by an air campaign carefully coordinated with the resurgent Northern Alliance. The Taliban's fanatical loyalty had crumbled with remarkable speed, as many simply switched sides, persuaded either by U.S. bombs or U.S. cash distributed through the North Alliance.

For some, this showed the hypercritical nature of the modern media. However, others looked at the coverage of the war and saw an entirely different bias. Far from being too negative, the media did not question the president's policy choices enough, according to some on the left. It is true that very few voices in the media ever questioned the necessity of the war. The networks in particular seemed to compete with one another to appear the most patriotic, wrapping their newscasts in jingoistic bursts of red, white, and blue. What is the appropriate role of the media in wartime? Should they support the government or just report the facts? Can they do both? Moreover, in an increasingly international media market, to what extent is, for example, the Cable News Network (CNN) an "American" network? Do viewers in other countries turn to CNN to get an American point of view? Would American viewers have punished any network that was insufficiently pro-American?

has inaugurated an era of low-casualty conflicts, at least in terms of U.S. deaths. Even the Persian Gulf War, the largest combat operation by the United States since Vietnam, resulted in few American deaths compared to previous conflicts. To be sure, presidents have not hesitated to use military force since Vietnam. The United States inflicted combat or civilian deaths on a long list of countries, including Libya, Grenada, Iran, Panama, Iraq, Serbia, Sudan, Somalia, and Afghanistan. Presidents have, however, avoided large-scale commitments of U.S. ground troops in war zones, preferring to use long-range missiles or American air power to bomb other countries in pursuit of U.S. policy.

President Bush, both in his September 20 speech to Congress and in his speech announcing hostilities with Afghanistan, warned that the war on terrorism would not be such a war, that it would involve U.S. casualties. However, the Bush battle plan showed a keen awareness that Americans, naturally, prefer to win wars without U.S. deaths. While polls showed the vast majority of Americans were willing to pursue war in Afghanistan even if it meant substantial U.S. casualties, Bush crafted a war that avoided testing whether the public was really cured of the Vietnam syndrome. First, Bush took on the Taliban from the air and with clandestine special forces. Next, the Northern Alliance, with heavy U.S. logistic support, began a slow ground offensive against the Taliban. At this point, the Bush war came under sharp domestic criticism. Bush stayed the course, refusing to order a large-scale ground invasion of Afghanistan as demanded by some of his critics. By December 18, scarcely six weeks after the war began, U.S.-supported troops had marched into Kabul and brought down the Taliban. The Northern Alliance, which had controlled barely 10 percent of the country on September 11, now controlled almost the entirety of the nation. Bush had won a victory with even fewer U.S. casualties than his father had in his defeat of Saddam Hussein in 1991.

While Bush cautioned that the war against terror was far from over and that al-Qaeda and other terrorist groups still operated around the world, it was clear that Bush and his military team had won a victory much quicker than many in America and around the world had anticipated. The public, which had not wavered in their support for the president during the weeks leading up to the attack or the six weeks of war, continued to approve of Bush at record levels.

BUSH'S STATE OF THE UNION: VOLUNTEERISM AGAINST THE "AXIS OF EVIL"

The Constitution commands that the president report to Congress from time to time on the state of the union. Since Woodrow Wilson's presidency, the State of the Union address has become a very formal occasion, in which the president travels to Capitol Hill personally and announces his agenda for the year. Bush's speech was given from a position of extraordinary strength. He had promised Congress on September 20 that the Taliban would either turn over bin Laden or fall, and he had deftly led a military campaign and a diplomatic coalition to fulfill his promise. None of the dire predictions of his critics occurred. The war in Afghanistan had not ignited the flames of anti-Americanism across the Islamic world, and allies in Egypt, Saudi Arabia, and Pakistan had not been unseated by outraged Muslim citizens.

Bush's speech bluntly cautioned the nation that while Afghanistan had been defeated, other nations were harboring terrorists and seeking to harm America. Bush's promise to take strong action against rogue nations developing weapons of mass destruction was a sobering reminder that many within his administration consider the war on Afghanistan merely the first act in a lengthy struggle. Bush labeled three nations—Iraq, Iran, and North Korea—an "Axis of Evil," a phrase designed to bring back memories of the World War II fascist axis of Germany, Italy, and Japan. Bush laid out his budget plans, calling for the largest increase in defense spending in a generation, and a 100 percent increase for homeland security. It was clear from the enthusiastic applause and standing ovation of the members of Congress that he would have bipartisan support in the war on terror and full funding for his initiatives. But Bush threw down the gauntlet to Democrats in the next section of his speech, when he pledged to resist any attempts to roll back his 10-year plan to cut taxes, narrowly passed the year before. Bush went further, arguing that the economic downturn since September 11 demanded billions more in new tax cuts, again largely benefiting wealthier Americans. Democrats charged that Bush was leading the country back into the days of massive deficits with his "reckless" tax cuts favoring the wealthiest 5 percent of the population, but Republicans received that portion of the speech with fervor.

Bush received bipartisan support for his "Freedom Corps" proposal, an idea to tap the reservoir of goodwill and community that had sprung up in the aftermath of September 11. First, Bush would expand AmeriCorps, a Clinton administration program that places volunteers with community groups at partial government expense. Bush suggested that many of the social problems of the day could be addressed by such groups, particularly those with religious ties. He also specifically called on seniors to lend their expertise to homeland defense in such areas as emergency response and medical care. Bush also called for a large expansion in the number of Peace Corps volunteers, specifically targeting the Middle East and the Islamic world. Bush's volunteerism initiative cleverly mingled conservative and liberal rhetoric. Many conservatives have long seen faith-based community groups as a way to address social needs without massive increases in government spending. Liberals have seen Clinton's AmeriCorps as a model program that enhances Americans' sense of citizenship and have also strongly supported the Peace Corps, a creation of a liberal icon, John F. Kennedy. Bush's plan built on legislation already under consideration by Senator John McCain, a key maverick Republican and sometime opponent of the president. Bush's plan did face criticism from right-wing Republicans, such as Majority Leader Dick Armey (R-Tex.), who had tried for years to end Clinton's AmeriCorps program. However, such intraparty opposition to a popular proposal put forward by a president at the zenith of his approval ratings was unlikely to succeed. Indeed, Bush's positioning on volunteerism was remarkably similar to Clinton's "triangulation" strategy of the 1990s, in which

Clinton almost relished the opposition of liberal Democrats to make him appear more moderate. The criticism from Armey and other conservative Republicans on Capitol Hill did not appear to threaten the chance of passage of the Freedom Corps, and it burnished Bush's image as a "compassionate conservative."

The State of the Union could be seen as the end of the first stage of Bush's response to the terrorist attacks of September 11. In many ways, Bush's response to the attacks was a personal triumph. Less than 10 months before the attacks, Bush was declared the winner of the ugliest and most contested presidential election since 1876. Millions of Americans had perceived him as a man who had won the presidency in a tainted fashion, through a partisan Supreme Court vote. Moreover, while most Americans liked Bush much better than they did his opponent, Al Gore, many harbored grave doubts about his abilities and his intellectual acumen. Among the areas that had attracted the greatest concern was Bush's lack of any foreign policy experience. During the campaign, he had failed to identify the leaders of India and Pakistan (leaders of vital importance in the weeks after September 11) and had at other times appeared underinformed across an array of international issues. Faced with America's gravest foreign policy crisis since 1941, Bush had had a lot to prove to many Americans. According to opinion polls and the commentary of Washington insiders, Bush had more than exceeded low expectations. Off the record, some prominent Democrats expressed relief that Gore had not been president, if only because Republicans in Congress would have never allowed him the time given Bush to craft a military plan and an international coalition.

Had Bush changed, or had the crisis merely allowed America to see the merits of the man they had so narrowly elected? Preeminent presidential scholar Fred Greenstein felt that the president had in fact changed: "I don't think he's any smarter today, but he is more up to speed. This is a man who now seems inclined to get into specifics. And what is behind that is a sense of mission." Faced with the awesome responsibility of leading the nation into the first war of the 21st century, George Walker Bush had become a better president.

2

❄

Congress in Crisis: Deference and Dissent

Chaos ruled Capitol Hill. Wild rumors passed as fact. A bomb had gone off at the Pentagon. More planes were heading toward the White House. The Air Force had shot down a jet headed for the Capitol. Unlike the executive branch, there was no evacuation plan put into effect. Vice President Cheney intervened and ordered that the leaders of Congress be taken to a secure location (rumored to be West Virginia). Later in the day, a Republican senator demanded in a call to Cheney that the leadership return to Washington so that Congress could convene. When Cheney refused, the senator pointed out that Congress was an independent branch of government, not under executive control. According to the *Washington Post,* Cheney calmly replied, "We control the helicopters."

Perhaps nothing better demonstrates the immediate increase in executive power in relation to Congress that occurs in any national crisis. The more severe and swift the crisis, the more executive power grows. On September 11, Congress demonstrated the wisdom of the Founding Fathers, who had placed a strong executive atop government in part so that the nation would not be leaderless in moments of sudden attack. Members of Congress could not figure out where to go, let alone what the nation's response should be. Some gathered at the front of the Capitol to pray with the Senate chaplain. Others went to the headquarters of the Capitol Hill police force. Many simply went home because rumors of a fourth plane headed toward Washington caused the evacuation of Congress. Perhaps Congress's lack of organization should not be surprising. After all, the executive branch had taken Congress's leaders off to a secret location for their safety.

Congress's first responses to the attacks signified its willingness to be led by the president in this moment of tragedy and danger. Yet that mood of submission would not last, nor would it be unanimous. Even in an unprecedented national crisis, the separation of powers, which pits, according to James Madison's design, "ambition versus ambition," would survive. The men and women of Congress would begin to question the actions of the executive, defeat at least two of his key initiatives, and demonstrate that the legislative branch would not surrender its constitutional prerogatives. Some in Congress would even challenge not only the executive but also the overwhelming tide of American public opinion.

CONGRESS AND CRISIS IN
A THEORETICAL CONTEXT

Throughout American history, the response of Congress to crises, particularly crises involving the military and international affairs, has been one of deference to the executive. There are four central reasons why Congress defers: constitutional design, tradition, lack of information and expertise, and public pressure.

As seen in Chapter 1, the president is far more dominant in foreign policy and military affairs than he is in domestic politics. While Congress could ultimately refuse to fund a foreign military adventure launched by the president, this is a rarity in American history, arguably occurring only once, when Congress refused President Ford's request to fund special assistance to the collapsing government of South Vietnam in 1975. The Supreme Court has also apparently given the president the power to abrogate treaties without Senate consent (in the case of *Goldwater v. Carter* [1979]), although some question whether this issue has been fully addressed by the courts. By making the president the sole commander of the armed forces, the Constitution prevents Congress from directly affecting the conduct of war. The president has also been seen as the leader of foreign policy, the representative of the nation overseas. When foreign and military issues are minor parts of the nation's agenda, as in the 1990s, we expect to see a president in a far weaker position in relation to Congress. In fact, Congress took on a greater leadership role in the 1990s, after the end of the Cold War, than it did in the 1970s and 1980s. The attacks of September 11 returned foreign policy and military questions to the center of the agenda, strengthening the presidency as an institution and George Bush as an individual.

The Constitution places greater power in foreign policy with the Senate than with the House. This is true not only because the Senate possesses the power to approve treaties with foreign governments but also because the Senate has the power to approve top government nominees. It is not unusual for a member of the Senate Foreign Relations Committee to place a hold on a nominee to a diplomatic position because the senator objects to some aspect of the administration's foreign policy. Senators are also more interested in foreign policy than House members because most senators represent many more constituents, who have more diverse foreign policy views than found in a typical House district. Finally, the Senate is far more likely to produce a presidential nominee than the House, and so those who catch "presidential fever" often take prominent positions on foreign policy

Congress Under Attack: Anthrax Shakes and Isolates the Congress

Following the delivery of anthrax-laden letters to media outlets in Florida in October, a suspicious letter was sent to Senate Majority Leader Daschle (D-S.D.). It contained a highly dangerous weaponized form of anthrax. House Minority Leader Richard Gephardt (D-Mo.) and Speaker of the House Dennis Hastert (R-Ill.), who were meeting with Bush at the White House, believed that the congressional leaders had agreed to adjourn Congress in the face of the threat. Hastert returned to the House and announced that in order to protect the safety of congressional staffers, the House was closing down. This announcement appalled some senators, who saw it as cowardice in the face of terrorism. They pressured Daschle and Senate Minority Leader Trent Lott (R-Miss.) to stay open, and at 1:00 P.M., Daschle announced that the Senate would not adjourn. House members were furious that their leaders had let them appear to be frightened while senators looked brave. Congress could not have appeared more divided and leaderless if it had tried. And the House's actions came under swift and brutal criticism. *Time* magazine bitterly and perhaps unfairly compared the behavior of Congress with that of the heroes of 9-11:

> *The standards by which we judge public servants changed on Sept. 11, and maybe the guys in Congress just never go the word. When buildings in New York City were targeted and ablaze, the firefighters just ran into them. Last week, when buildings in Washington were targeted, the House members left town. While Senators camped in cubby holes and went about their business, Congressmen called it a day and adjourned. They forgot that in wartime, symbols have substance: no war—not World War II, not World War I, not the Civil War, not even the War of 1812, when British forces burned the White House—has forced the U.S. Congress to evacuate. But that has happened twice in the past*

five weeks: after the Sept. 11 attack and then again last Thursday.

In response to such criticism, Gephardt defended his actions: "What message would it send to the terrorists if we stupidly put people back in harm's way, to be infected by anthrax?" But the anthrax scare changed the way Congress operated for months. Several office buildings had to be shut down and painstakingly fumigated. Members of Congress were forced to share cramped office quarters. All mail to Congress was delayed for weeks. Hundreds of staffers were put on powerful antibiotics. It reminded Congress that in the war on terror, they were as much on the front line as any American citizen. It also contributed to congressional deference to the president since the normal operations of the Congress had been so disrupted.

The FBI remains baffled as to who is responsible for the anthrax mailings. Some of the fragmentary evidence suggests that it is the work of domestic terrorists or even a solitary disgruntled scientist. Whoever is responsible certainly raised the level of fear on Capitol Hill. Members of Congress are taking no chances with security. New measures went into effect almost immediately. Not only is all mail to Congress irradiated to kill potential biohazards, but Congress itself is more physically isolated than ever before. Security checkpoints designed to stop truck bombers or gunmen now surround the Capitol. And the majestic views from the balconies of the Capitol, which had been open to tourists since the construction of the building, are now inaccessible. If the Capitol is intended to be a symbol of democracy, what does it say about democracy that the people's business must be conducted behind heavy security?

issues in order to seem presidential. However, the greater power granted to the Senate in foreign affairs diminishes in national crises. Treaty approval and confirmation hearings are rare events in the heat of a crisis.

The tradition of deference to the president in foreign crises emerged early in American history and has grown over time. In 1793, as war raged in Europe between France and Britain, President Washington issued the Neutrality Proclamation, setting the foreign policy of the United States without consulting Congress.

Nowhere in the Constitution is the president given such power to unilaterally set doctrines to guide our foreign affairs, and indeed, Madison himself protested that Washington's action was invalid because only Congress had authority over war and peace. However, others see such acts by presidents as logical consequences of certain implied and inherent powers in the presidency, comparable to the Supreme Court's implied power of judicial review. Since Washington, presidents have announced the policy of the United States on various crucial matters, perhaps most famously in the issuance of the Monroe Doctrine, in which European powers were warned not to involve themselves too deeply in the Western Hemisphere. Other important proclamations include the Truman Doctrine (pledging the United States to contain communist infiltration of Europe) and the Reagan Doctrine (pledging to roll back Soviet gains in the Third World and elsewhere). While Congress could challenge such broad presidential policies, they are usually hesitant to do so.

Congress also defers to the president because it lacks the information and expertise to challenge him in crises. The president is aware of important shifts in international affairs before Congress in many cases through his access to secret intelligence, embassy reports, and the opinions of foreign leaders. Each morning, the president receives a briefing from the director of the CIA, updating him on any developments that occurred while he slept. Congress must wait for the executive branch to decide what information is passed along. Often, presidents resist giving secret data to Congress for fear that it will be leaked. Even when presidents do provide timely intelligence to Congress, access to the most important secrets is usually limited to the four congressional leaders or the members of the intelligence committees. Finally, members of Congress often arrive in Washington with expertise and interests in many aspects of domestic policy, but few members of Congress bring similar experiences in foreign policy to office. By contrast, presidents often arrive in the White House with vast experiences in foreign affairs. When George H. W. Bush took office in 1989, he had served as director of the CIA as well as ambassador to China and the United Nations. President Eisenhower had directed the Allied war effort against the Nazis and knew many world leaders personally. In selecting a president, the public is far more likely to care about foreign policy views and experience than it is in electing members of Congress. When it comes to international crises, knowledge is power, and the president simply has much more of it.

The public also plays a role in causing congressional deference. In normal periods, the public contributes to congressional inattention to foreign policy. Few citizens contact members about foreign policy questions, and foreign affairs seldom enters into congressional campaigns. In crises, the public exerts pressure on Congress to defer to presidential leadership, put aside personal agendas and partisan "bickering," and work together to provide the president with united support.

In deferring to the president in crises, Congress tends to act in a unified manner, very unlike the fragmented and contentious nature of normal politics on Capitol Hill. (A similar pattern appears during crises in parliamentary systems when a "government of national unity" brings most parties into power.) Many congressional experts see the most important question at any given moment as the degree of centralization or decentralization in the operations of Congress. Compared to the legislatures of most countries, the U.S. Congress is highly decentralized. Decentralizing forces include elections, campaign fund-raising, personal beliefs, interest groups, and the eternal split between the two houses. Centralizing forces can include the leadership, shared ideology, regionalism, and a popular president. But no force in congressional politics centralizes like a war or national crisis. Beneath the surface unity, however, lurk the forces of party, ideology, interest groups, and personal ambition that divide Congress from the president in normal times. These decentralizing agents emerge as the crisis recedes, as happened with the attacks of September 11.

THE INITIAL CONGRESSIONAL RESPONSE:
NEARLY UNANIMOUS DEFERENCE

There was little doubt in the days after September 11 that President Bush would receive support from Congress for nearly any use of force short of nuclear retaliation. The mood on Capitol Hill reflected the mood of the nation as a whole: angry, bellicose, and resolute. Congress, like the country, sought to rally behind the president. Indeed, the only scenario in which Congress might have refused to defer to the president would have been if Bush had sought to make peace with those who brought down the World Trade Center towers. In the fantastical event that Bush had rejected the use of force following the first assault on American soil in more than a generation, it is conceivable that Congress would have moved to impeach him for violating his oath of office and his Article II duties under the Constitution. Absent that hypothetical occurrence, congressional deference was almost a given.

When Congress considered a resolution authorizing a military response, it passed immediately and almost unanimously. The language contained few limits on presidential discretion. If, for example, evidence had emerged that al-Qaeda had been operating out of Iran and/or Iraq, the congressional resolution provided all the authority Bush needed to launch a war far larger than the one in Afghanistan. It was essentially a blank check, unlike any Congress had given a president since the Gulf of Tonkin Resolution in 1964. It demonstrated Congress's responsiveness to the public mood and the willingness of the legislative branch to follow Bush wherever he might lead.

Aside from the solitary dissent of Congresswoman Barbara Lee, who voted against the use-of-force resolution, bipartisan support for the president was widespread in the days following the attacks. Congress appeared on the television screens of the nation, singing (somewhat off key) "God Bless America," a strong demonstration of unity if not harmony. As Bush left the podium after his September 20 speech, he fulsomely hugged Senate Majority Leader Tom Daschle (D-S.D.), who only weeks before had been demonized by the White House for blocking the nation's agenda. Bush also hugged Richard Gephardt (D-Mo.), the House minority leader, a strong partisan Democrat who had worked hard against Bush's cherished tax cuts. After the speech, there was no response from the

The Use-of-Force Resolution

SEC. 2. AUTHORIZATION FOR USE OF UNITED STATES ARMED FORCES.

(a) IN GENERAL—That the President is authorized to use all necessary and appropriate force against those nations, organizations, or persons he determines planned, authorized, committed, or aided the terrorist attacks that occurred on September 11, 2001, or harbored such organizations or persons, in order to prevent any future acts of international terrorism against the United States by such nations, organizations or persons.

(b) War Powers Resolution Requirements—

(1) SPECIFIC STATUTORY AUTHORIZATION— Consistent with section 8(a)(1) of the War Powers Resolution, the Congress declares that this section is intended to constitute specific statutory authorization within the meaning of section 5(b) of the War Powers Resolution.

Some analysts felt that the use-of-force resolution granted too much power to the president. As written, the resolution does give the power to the president to expand hostilities far beyond Afghanistan without the need for further congressional action. It is entirely at the president's discretion to attack, for example, Iraq or Iran if he determines that they were involved in any fashion with the attacks of September 11. Although Congress did once again assert the relevance of the War Powers Act as it passed this resolution, it failed to place any meaningful limits on Bush's ability to decide where to wage the war on terror. This may be the reason that Bush chose to seek a use-of-force resolution instead of a formal declaration of war. A declaration of war would have to specify the nations to be fought. The use-of-force resolution offers far more flexibility.

opposition party, as is traditional with the State of the Union and the weekly presidential radio address. Rather, the leaders of Congress appeared together to embrace the president's plans for the nation. Between Bush's hugs and the unified leadership response, the message was conveyed to the nation that the two elected branches of government were united and that Congress was following the president.

The interbranch cooperation did not end on September 20. Senator Carl Levin (D-Mich.) had been planning to block aspects of Bush's missile defense plan but for the sake of unity put his legislation aside. Republicans temporarily put away plans for a new capital gains tax cut because they felt it was likely to lead to a divisive partisan vote in Congress. But the most important bipartisan behavior was taking place at the highest levels of Congress. For weeks following September 11, a "Gang of Five" composed of the president, Daschle, Gephardt, Senate Minority Leader Trent Lott (R-Miss.), and Speaker of the House Denny Hastert (R-Ill.) met at the White House for breakfast every Tuesday or Wednesday at 7:00 A.M. No aides were permitted to attend these private meetings, although Vice President Cheney joined the five on occasion, and several cabinet secretaries made presentations. At these breakfasts, the president worked out the broad outlines of a supplemental appropriations bill and emergency assistance legislation to help the airlines. Not only were the leaders of Congress working with the president in a way unprecedented in modern memory, but the congressional leadership was negotiating directly as had not been common since the decentralizing reforms of the early 1970s at least.

Refusing to Defer: Congressional Dissenters in Crises

Representative Barbara Lee (D-Calif.) was the lone dissenting vote against the resolution authorizing President Bush's use of force against those who attacked America. Lee briefly became one of the most reviled figures in American politics.

The vote on the use-of-force resolution in Congress on September 14 reflected the bipartisan support for President Bush among the nation's legislators: 98 to 0 in the Senate and 420 to 1 in the House. The only person to vote against the resolution, Representative Barbara Lee (D-Calif.), called her act "a vote of conscience." Her decision raises an important question: What is the role of an elected representative? Should they vote as the people wish (delegate), or should they vote according to their personal conscience (trustee)?

In Lee's speech on the floor, she said, "I am convinced that military action will not prevent further acts of international terrorism against the United States . . . let us not become the evil we deplore." As soon as the public became aware of her vote, the Capitol Hill telephone system was flooded with protests, and Lee was placed under 24-hour police protection because of numerous threats to her life.

Throughout American history, there have been those in Congress who resisted deferring to the president in moments of crisis. In 1941, Senator Jeannette Rankin (R-Mont.) cast the only vote against the declaration of war against Japan. Rankin's vote, in the aftermath of the sneak attack on Pearl Harbor, made her the object of public scorn and death threats. Rankin had also been one of 56 House members to vote against the entry of the United States into World War I in 1917. In 1964, Senators Ernest Gruening (D-Alaska) and Wayne Morse (D-Ore.) were the only two votes against the Tonkin Gulf Resolution authorizing the expanded use of force in Vietnam.

The fate of these three dissenters may help explain why Congress defers to the president in times of crisis. Morse and Gruening lost their reelection bids; their votes against the war helped lead to their defeats. Rankin, facing an outraged electorate, left the Senate rather than run again. If political scientist David Mayhew is correct, and reelection is the prime directive of every member of Congress, the lesson of history is clear: Do not dissent in crisis. However, in another sense, the longer view of history has been kinder to all three dissenters. Morse and Gruening ultimately saw their suspicions of the Tonkin Gulf Resolution verified. It was later revealed that President Johnson had greatly exaggerated the clash with North Vietnam that he used to justify military action, saying, "For all I know, our Navy was shooting at whales out there!" The reputations of Morse and Gruening improved as the Vietnam War worsened. In Rankin's case, a statue of her now sits in the Capitol. President Kennedy, long after the passions of war had died down, said of Rankin, "Few members of Congress have ever stood more alone while being true to higher honor and loyalty."

Will Lee be defeated in 2002? Her district—Berkeley, California—is perhaps the most pacifist in the country, but even there her vote was controversial. It is possible that a fourth name will be added to the list of those who swam against a national mood for war and paid for their dissent with their seats in Congress.

The four congressmen were getting to know one another as people, a rare but crucial development in the time-pressured and highly partisan modern Congress. Before the 1970s, it was routine for members of Congress to socialize across party lines, to get to know one another as individuals. Congressional leaders such as Everett Dirksen, Lyndon Johnson, Gerald Ford, and Tip O'Neil knew each other quite well despite their ideological and partisan differences. In recent times, because airline travel has made it easier for members to live away from Washington and because fund-raising places heavy demands on their time, members simply do not have the kind of personal relationships that made congressional compromises easier in the past. Congressional scholars have even blamed the loss of personal connections among members for the increasingly bitter partisan mood in Congress. The bonding among the four congressional leaders began on September 11, when they were isolated for their security. As Gephardt told the *Philadelphia Inquirer,* "We were in this room together and spent more time together than we've probably spent in our lives together. When there are four people in a foxhole, you learn a lot from each other."

However, rank-and-file Democrats and Republicans grew increasingly unhappy with the bipartisan mood of contentment. Fissures began to appear in the unity on Capitol Hill as Republicans on the right and Democrats on the left began to suspect that their leaders were cutting too many deals without their input.

THE LIMITS OF BIPARTISANSHIP:
BUSH LOSES TWO BATTLES ON CAPITOL HILL

One of the first items on Congress's agenda following the passage of the emergency airline bailout legislation was airport security. The 19 al-Qaeda hijackers had passed through security and boarded four commercial flights without incident. Polls of the American public showed that many harbored fears of flying in the aftermath of September 11. Even after the nation's airports reopened, air traffic was greatly reduced. To address the people's concerns, Congress began to examine how airport security could be improved. The media was full of stories of airport security attendants making less than the fast-food restaurant employees at the same airports. Critics wondered why the person ensuring that their McNuggets were heated should make more than the person ensuring that their planes were not hijacked. The turnover at some airport screening jobs was well over 80 percent. Training was reported to be haphazard and security breaches frequent. Boston's Logan Airport, where one of the hijackings occurred, had had leaky security for years, as was well known to the Transportation Department. The *Atlanta Journal Constitution* found that Atlanta's airport had had 759 security breaches since 1997, 249 involving undetected handguns and 5 involving undetected rifles. The turnover among airport security approached an extraordinary 375 percent a year in Atlanta, perhaps because the starting salary was just $7 an hour.

For many congressional Democrats, the problem was simple: private contractors who submitted the lowest bid to airport authorities and tried, naturally, to increase their profits by cutting corners and using unskilled employees. They immediately suggested federalizing airport security and creating a new agency under the Department of Transportation to hire and train professional screeners who would be better paid. Legislation calling for this, as well as improvements in airport screening equipment, passed the Senate 100 to 0 in the weeks after September 11. However, House Republicans took a dim view of expanding federal employment. They supported new standards for screeners, such as higher salaries and better training, but wanted to allow private companies to continue to provide the employees. Republicans pointed out that certain aspects of airport security in Europe and Israel were performed by private companies. Republicans also warned that federal screeners would be almost impossible to fire for incompetence because federal employees enjoy almost total job security under civil service rules. The Bush administration supported the House Republicans, and the bill to federalize airport screening died in the House, where the Republicans narrowly passed their version of airport security legislation. A conference committee composed of representatives and senators then met to iron out the differences between the House and Senate bills.

Why did the post–September 11 bipartisan unity break down on federalizing airport security? The issue exposed long-standing ideological and interest group divisions between Democrats and Republicans. Democrats have, since F.D.R., tended to favor federal solutions to important problems. Additionally, Democrats receive huge sums of campaign donations from the unions of federal employees. Federal employees also tend to vote Democratic, in part because that is often the party seeking to expand, or at least preserve, the size of the federal workforce. An estimated 20,000 to 40,000 new federal employees, spread across the country, would be a small but real boost to Democratic campaign coffers and electoral chances. Republicans, by contrast, tend to favor local or state solutions to problems such as airport security. They also put greater trust in private corporations than they do in federal bureaucracies. Finally, Republicans receive far more corporate money than do Democrats.

Although Bush lobbied hard in opposition to full federalization of airport security, the Democrats had a potent weapon in their favor: public opinion. Polls consistently showed that the American public would feel safer if federal employees were responsible for screening passengers and baggage. Embarrassing stories of mistakes and private firms hiring numerous convicted felons percolated throughout the media during the deadlock. Then American Airlines Flight 587 crashed in Queens, New York. Although the crash turned out to have nothing to do with airport security or terrorism, it seemed to galvanize public opinion toward swift action to ensure airline safety. The pressure grew too great, and the Bush administration and House Republicans caved to the Democratic plan for federalization. The Republicans did win a few points in the compromise legislation. The federal screeners, unlike most federal employees, would face immediate dismissals for malfeasance and incompetence. While all 419 U.S. airports that fly commercial airliners would have to use federal screeners, after a few years airports would be allowed to "opt out" and hire private companies to do the work if they wished. However, the likelihood of an airport authority taking such a step in the face of public concern over terrorism was considered low. The Democrats had taken on Bush when his public approval was at a record high and won a near-total victory.

An even more bitter battle had been taking place over a "stimulus" package to provide immediate economic assistance. Stimulus packages are supplemental legislation designed to bring a short-term boost to the nation's economy, usually to stave off or shorten a recession. The Democratic-controlled Senate Finance Committee passed by one vote a bill that extended unemployment benefits by 13 weeks, gave a healthcare subsidy to workers who lost their jobs as a result of the attacks, provided a $300 tax rebate to low-income workers, and extended certain business tax incentives. The Republican House also passed a bill that would extend unemployment benefits but accompanied them with large new tax cuts on top of Bush's 10-year tax reduction plan. These tax cuts, like Bush's, also gave the majority of their benefits to the wealthiest segment of society. For example, the Republicans proposed an immediate end to the estate tax, a tax that in its current form applied only to millionaires and billionaires. The Senate was unable to come to any agreement on final stimulus legislation. Senate rules required at least 60 votes to pass such a bill, and with the partisan split in the chamber being 50 Democrats, 49 Republicans, and 1 independent (Vermont Senator Jim Jeffords), neither party could muster enough support for its stimulus package. The Senate recessed for the holiday break without passing a bill. Bush's State of the Union speech in late January called on the Senate to pass the bill, and the Bush administration worked long hours to try to forge a compromise. The Senate remained divided, and the stimulus legislation ultimately died in early February.

Why did Congress fail to pass a stimulus bill much desired by an extraordinarily popular president? The Republican and Democratic plans were very far apart from the start, reflecting the ideological positions of the parties since the New Deal era. Republicans wanted to stimulate the economy with tax cuts tilted toward upper income brackets, believing that the rich would reinvest their money in the economy and the benefits would trickle down to the lower classes. The Democrats preferred new spending combined with tax breaks aimed at the working class. Republicans also feared that providing subsidized health care for laid-off workers would set a precedent for nationalizing health care in the near future. The Senate Democrats loaded up their stimulus package with numerous pork-barrel benefits for specific states, much to the dismay of Republicans. The prospect of midterm elections in November 2002 was also crucial. Republicans were quite willing to let the stimulus package die, as long as they could blame its death on the intransigence of Tom Daschle and the Senate Democrats. If the economic downturn deepened and persisted into the election season, Republicans could implicate congressional Democrats. Perhaps most important, the economy itself showed faint signs of recovery by early 2002, thus lessening the public pressure for congressional economic assistance.

The failure of Bush to get his way in Congress on airport security and with the stimulus package illustrates that congressional deference to the president in crises situations has distinct limits. First, the nearer in time to the crisis, the more likely the president is to get his way. By the time of the final stimulus negotiations, al-Qaeda and the Taliban were on the run, and there had been no further anthrax attacks. Second, the issues on which Bush was defeated were domestic ones. Bush's foreign policy and military initiatives have received broad bipartisan support in the months since September 11.

CONGRESS AND SPENDING: THE RETURN OF DEFICIT POLITICS

From 1981 to 1997, Congress's behavior was heavily influenced by the massive increases in federal deficits that took place in the early Reagan administration. As the national debt (the accumulated annual deficits) grew almost $3 trillion, the amount of the federal budget that went to pay interest on that debt increased each year. This put pressure on discretionary spending, particularly in domestic programs. Congress could not easily launch new programs. From the late 1980s on, Congress had to "pay as you go," or "Paygo," by specifying where exactly the budget would be cut to provide the money for new initiatives. This created a "zero-sum politics" of winners and losers, far different from the 1950s and 1960s, when it seemed that federal revenues would increase almost inevitably and hard spending choices could be avoided. The deficit had broader implications as well. Many economists worried that the long-term effects of running massive deficits would be high interest rates and low economic growth. In the late Bush and early Clinton administrations, the deficit was attacked directly, and by 1997 the U.S. government was operating at a surplus for the first time in decades. The brief era of surplus politics had profound effects on American government. Funding for a number of domestic programs, such as education, grew far faster than the rate of inflation. Congressional candidates could talk again about huge new spending programs, such as guaranteeing cheap prescription drugs to seniors. The presidential campaign of 2000 and many congressional races revolved around what Congress would do with the trillions of dollars in surplus government revenues expected by 2010. Should the money go to pay down the accumulated debt? Should it go into Al Gore's "lockbox" and be saved to meet the retirement expenses of the baby-boomer generation, the largest in American history? Or should a significant portion of it be returned to the people in the form of tax cuts, as the Republicans n Congress advocated? Working with the president, Republicans enacted a 10-year tax cut plan that reduced but did not eliminate the federal surplus. Based on optimistic projections, the surplus era in Congress was not yet over.

The attacks of September 11 ended surplus politics for the foreseeable future. The Congress now faces deficits for at least the next four years and quite possibly much longer. Public opinion polls suggest that Americans do not care how much money security costs—they will pay for it. As in World War II and most previous military conflicts, government expenditures are expected to rise. If this means a deficit and the inability to take certain beneficial actions, then so be it, declare Congress and the polls. Congress and the president have both warned the people that the war on terror demands sacrifices and that prior wars have usually ended with the government running a substantial deficit. But unlike the Civil War,

World War I, World War II, the Korean War, and the Vietnam War, Congress has not asked the public to sacrifice by raising taxes to pay for at least part of this war, instead relying entirely on future generations to foot the new spending. Congress, which under the Constitution holds the power of the purse, has made a clear choice to return to the much-criticized era of large deficits. Why did bipartisanship on Capitol Hill not produce a "war tax" to partially cover the military costs of conflict? First, and most important, Bush, unlike previous wartime presidents, firmly opposed any new taxes. But the tensions between the parties in Congress played a key role as well. Most Republicans in Congress are ideologically opposed to tax increases because they believe that Americans are already taxed at far too high a rate, particularly the wealthy. They see tax cuts as the solution to recessions and believe that they are just as necessary in good economic times. Democrats, burned by the experience of endorsing tax increases in the 1980s, are loath to go to the American public as the party of higher taxes. In a time of crisis, these partisan and ideological forces do not magically vanish. The logical outcome of crisis expenses and gridlock on taxes was the immediate disappearance of the vaunted surplus and the reappearance of massive deficits. Among the bipartisan choices Congress made after September 11, the nearly unanimous choice to avoid new taxes may have the longest effect on the way Congress legislates and the nation's economy.

CONGRESS AND CRISIS: EMERGING CONFLICT, EVENTUAL REASSERTION OF POWERS?

The deference that Congress showed to President Bush in the days and weeks following September 11 did not vanish, but it had become, by March 2002, much less of a force in congressional politics. Similar patterns have occurred in prior crises. Congress willingly granted President Roosevelt nearly everything he asked for in the weeks after December 7, 1941, but as scandals involving bureaucratic and corporate abuses of the mammoth new war budget emerged, Congress began to hound the administration with investigations, even during wartime. When in late 2001 the Bush administration was rocked by murky allegations of ties to the collapse of Enron, the largest corporate bankruptcy in American history, Democrats did not wait long to begin investigations amidst the war on terror. The Enron scandal has yet to seriously weaken President Bush, who remains personally popular with the public and unconnected directly to any misdeeds. However, the response of Congress to Enron suggests that deference in crisis never implies a lengthy surrender of the constitutional prerogatives of the legislative branch.

Still, the deference shown to the president in security and military matters will continue. In early February, Congress announced a highly unusual joint intelligence committee to investigate the very touchy question of whether our intelligence agencies should have anticipated the September 11 attacks. Democrats in the Senate and Republicans in the House, who would normally lead such investigations, are instead sharing the spotlight to minimize partisan maneuvering. Should further terrorist acts occur or should Bush expand the war on terror to new nations, a new mood of deference will surely characterize congressional behavior for as long as the crisis lasts. Yet the forces of ambition, tradition, and ideology will eventually reemerge and return power to Congress. As intended by the Founders, the personal ambitions of members of Congress will act to preserve separation of powers, even in the aftermath of crisis.

Historically, Congress waits for crises to come to completion and then takes back large amounts of power. No president took more liberties with the Constitution than did Lincoln. After the Civil War, Congress impeached his successor and reasserted Congress's dominant policymaking role. Following World War I, Congress refused to approve President Wilson's League of Nations, a personal and institutional defeat that led to 12 years of weak presidents and strong Congresses. Even after Roosevelt's presidency, signs of congressional rebellion were present. To prevent any future president from taking so much personal power, the postwar Congress passed the 22d Amendment, limiting all future presidents to two terms in office. Given these historical examples, in the long run, it seems likely that Congress will once again establish its constitutional prerogatives after the war on terror ends.

3

✵

Civil Liberties in Crisis:
An Altered Balance

The FBI knew that they had something, but they were not sure what. They had arrested Zacarias Moussaoui, a French citizen of Moroccan descent, for violating his visa in early August 2001. They suspected he was connected to al-Qaeda, but they did not have firm proof. Moussaoui had been enrolled in a Minnesota flight school and had attracted the suspicion of his instructors because he wanted to practice only on jumbo jets and wanted only to practice flying, not taking off or landing. The FBI, after detaining him, wanted to search his computer and applied to the Justice Department for a warrant. Under the Fourth Amendment, the government may not conduct searches in most circumstances without a warrant, issued by a legal authority, specifying exactly what is to be searched, what the government expects to find, and why the government is searching the belongings or residence of a specific person or company. The FBI's request was denied because the justification for it was too weak and fragmentary. At the moment the first plane hit the World Trade Center, the FBI was contemplating sending Moussaoui to France, where authorities were less restricted by constitutional niceties and might be able to figure out who he was and what he had been planning. September 11, however, provided more than enough grounds for a warrant. The next day, when the FBI looked at his computer, they found evidence that might have led them to suspect that al-Qaeda was planning a large operation involving hijacking airplanes. Did a strict interpretation of the Fourth Amendment prevent the FBI from stopping the terrorist attacks that brought so much suffering and death to America?

Or consider another complaint made by FBI agents in the days after September 11. Since the 1970s, the FBI and other police agencies have been strictly limited in their ability to infiltrate political and religious organizations. Did this limit on the FBI prevent them from doing their job in the fight against terror? September 11 was not the first time forces linked to Osama bin Laden had attacked the World Trade Center. In 1993, a team of terrorists had detonated a rental truck loaded with explosives in an attempt to collapse one of the towers. Though the primitive attack killed only six persons, it injured thousands and suggested that Islamic radicals were capable of bold domestic attacks against American institutions. While those immediately responsible were ultimately arrested, tried, and convicted, the FBI was frustrated in its desire to infiltrate the Islamic religious organizations that seemed to have some connection to the event. The 1970s rules on surveillance and infiltration of domestic political and religious groups passed by Congress may have prevented America's police agencies from anticipating and preventing the horrors of September 11.

It is easy to blame America's broad constitutional protections for leaving the nation open to terrorist attacks. One of the inescapable costs of freedom in an open society is vulnerability to domestic enemies. It is, however, important to remember why the Fourth Amendment was written and why Congress limited infiltration of domestic groups. History has shown that unless limits on police and prosecutors, such as search warrants and probable cause, are enforced, government abuse of its enormous powers is the inevitable result. The infiltration rules were passed following revelations in congressional investigations that the government had unlawfully infiltrated anti-war and pro−civil rights groups. In the name of protecting the nation's security, agents had violated the privacy of American citizens, encouraged extreme acts of violence, and raised questions about the nature of America's republican government. Congress decided that the FBI and other agencies could not be trusted with this power, based on their past behavior.

Balancing the needs of government to provide security against the value of individual liberties is always difficult and always related to the circumstances. The attacks of September 11 changed the way Americans thought about their liberties and altered that delicate balance between order and liberty.

CIVIL LIBERTIES AND CRISIS IN A THEORETICAL CONTEXT

Civil liberties come under their greatest attack during wartime and crises. While the words of the Constitution do not seem to allow for much alteration during national emergencies, the courts have been far more lenient in interpreting the scope of government power during such times. An act that would be unconstitutional in peacetime may often be upheld in war. In many ways, this is simply logical. Consider the important constitutional principle "probable cause," which limits the ability of the government to arrest and search suspects. The government's suspicions about an odd airline pilot of Middle Eastern descent did not rise to the level of probable cause before September 11; afterward, they did. The Constitution did not change; what changed was the nature of the threat.

Civil libertarians often resist this logic, arguing that it is precisely during times of national emergency when civil liberties most desperately must be defended. When, for example, is freedom of speech more vital than in wartime? When Congress is deciding the appropriate level of agricultural subsidies, the right to criticize the government may not seem to be of supreme importance. When Congress is about to vote on sending young men and women off to die or when the forces of the nation are already engaged in war, the right to object to the government's conduct may be a matter of life and death. Do Americans lose freedoms precisely at the moment when they most need them?

Civil liberties, as upheld by a watchful judiciary, protect us not only against the government but also against the forces of government and civil society allied together, giving in to the angry moods so common during wars and crises. Other than in its treatment of African Americans during the long horror of slavery and Jim Crow, when has the right to equal protection been more seriously violated than in the way communities and the federal government treated Japanese Americans during World War II? During crises, the popular commitment to civil liberties, never as strong as civil libertarians would wish, often falls dramatically. Even in peacetime, many Americans indicate in surveys that they do not believe in the rights of certain minorities to have freedom of speech, whether that minority is pornographers, communists, or the Ku Klux Klan. In war, Americans have even less tolerance for dissent. The elected branches of government may easily be swayed by a popular mood in favor of constricting civil liberties in the name of security. Unfortunately, the unelected branch, the judiciary, may be of little help in crises. As constitutional expert John Frank concludes, "The dominant lesson of our history . . . is that courts love liberty most when it is under pressure least."

In the final analysis, it should be recalled that the preamble to the Constitution ordains that among the first obligations of government are to provide for the common defense, ensure domestic tranquility, and promote the general welfare as well as to secure the blessings of liberty. The idea that the most vital aim of government is the safety of the people is older than our Constitution. In the classic model of social contract theory articulated by such diverse thinkers as John Locke and Thomas Hobbes, citizens surrender certain limited rights to a government in order to receive protection for their persons and property. As the threat to security rises, this may justify government limiting other rights that in safer times are never violated. As *Time* essayist Lance Morrow argued, "A rattlesnake loose in the living room tends to end any discussion of animal rights." This does not mean that those who zealously fight for civil liberties are wrong to worry about government abuses in crises. In *1984,* George Orwell's brilliant novel depicting a totalitarian future, the state continually justifies its brutal treatment of its citizens by citing war and security threats. Or, as Supreme Court Justice Frank Murphy put it, "Few indeed have been the invasions upon essential liberties which have not been accompanied by pleas of urgent necessity advanced in good faith by responsible men." In every major crisis in American history, the question of how much freedom we must sacrifice in the name of security has arisen. The civil liberties issues that arose following September 11 were particularly interesting because of the domestic nature of the threat and the new technologies available to both terrorists and the U.S. government.

The History of Civil Liberties in Crises

Whenever America has found itself in moments of high national peril, the scope of the people's civil liberties has been lessened. Sometimes, it is clear the government has gone too far.

President Adams and the Alien and Sedition Acts

Although no war was taking place during John Adams's sole term in office (1797–1801), tensions were high in the country between those who supported the British in their conflicts with France and those who saw France as a revolutionary ally of the young United States. Adams and his Federalist Party allies in Congress passed the Alien and Sedition Acts, severely limiting criticism of the government, allegedly to avoid inflammatory rhetoric that might involve the United States in hostilities. The acts were used to imprison journalists who criticized Adams and the Federalist Congress, particularly journalists sympathetic to the Jeffersonian Republicans. James Madison and Thomas Jefferson, among others, fiercely opposed Adams, arguing that freedom of speech and association had been unnecessarily and unconstitutionally constrained. Three of the four acts were repealed or expired after Jefferson took office in 1801.

President Lincoln and Criticism in War

In addition to suspending habeas corpus (discussed in Chapter 1), Lincoln ordered military detentions for hundreds of suspected Confederate sympathizers, including 31 members of the Maryland legislature and an Ohio congressman. Al-though these actions were ruled unconstitutional by Chief Justice Roger Taney, Lincoln ignored the order. Later, Lincoln shut down newspapers that were too critical of the war effort. While Lincoln's actions may be subjected to severe criticism, they should also be understood in the context of the gravest threat to the nation's existence in the 212-year history of the union.

Limits During World War I

World War I was a conflict that many Americans opposed. Isolationists believed that the United States should stay out of a bloody and pointless war among European powers where no vital U.S. interests were at stake. German Americans were the largest ethnic group in the population, and many hesitated to support a war against their mother country. Many socialists and unionists also opposed the war, as did anarchists and pacifists. The government took aggressive actions against domestic critics of the war, imprisoning socialist leaders and those who advocated resisting the draft. The Supreme Court upheld the restrictions on free speech in the famous "fire in a crowded theater" case (*Schenck v. United States*). Justice Oliver Wendell Holmes, normally one of the stronger defenders of civil liberties, wrote for the Court that in wartime much was permitted that would not be allowed in peace. However, the postwar Palmer Raids, in which more than 6,000 "subversives" were rounded up for various minor charges, showed that the effects of wartime limitations on civil liberties could linger.

THE ROUNDUP: ASHCROFT ACTS AGAINST TERROR SUSPECTS AND WITNESSES

The first response of the Justice Department to the atrocities of September 11 was predictable: an attempt to locate those responsible and those with information about the attack. It was clear that the attacks had been conducted with careful planning over several years. Although those immediately responsible had been incinerated along with their victims, the FBI, working with our intelligence agencies and the resources of allied nations, was confident that such a large conspiracy had required cooperation and guidance from others. Were co-conspirators still in the United States? Even more important, al-Qaeda promised that more attacks

The History of Civil Liberties in Crises (*continued*)

Many were deported to Russia with little justification.

The Japanese Internment: American Concentration Camps for a Racial Minority

The attack on Pearl Harbor exacerbated existing anti-Japanese prejudices, particularly on the West Coast. Local authorities and the federal government ordered curfews and travel restrictions for the Japanese and ended up herding hundreds of thousands of Japanese Americans and Japanese residents into concentration camps far from the coast. The stated reason was fear of Japanese sabotage. The imprisonment lasted for years, although there was no evidence of a single Japanese American committing sabotage. Indeed, to the contrary, many young men from the camps volunteered for military service and demonstrated extraordinary bravery in the fight against Hitler in Europe at the same time that their families were prisoners in America. The imprisonment of the Japanese was upheld by the Supreme Court, again on the grounds that in war the other branches of government must trust the executive to know the threat best. A final irony was that German Americans were allowed complete freedom, although there was, in fact, evidence of at least one German American participating in sabotage against the United States.

Decades after the war, the U.S. government formally apologized to the internees and made substantial cash payments to these victims of wartime hysteria and racial prejudice.

McCarthyism and the Anti-Communist Hysteria

During the 1950s, there was a great fear of internal subversion and spying by Communists. The successful explosion by the Soviet Union of an atomic bomb and later a hydrogen bomb seemed to bring the threat of war home to many Americans. The fact that Soviet spies had stolen our nuclear secrets contributed to American fears of the "enemy within." The most populous nation in the world, China, had become Communist, and for much of this period America was fighting the forces of Red China in the Korean War. A demagogic senator, Joseph McCarthy (R-Wis.), made wild, unsubstantiated charges against individuals and institutions, linking them to a Communist conspiracy. So destructive were his attacks that he has come to symbolize the whole movement, which now goes by the name of "McCarthyism." But the threat to civil liberties was far broader than the grandstanding of one senator. Citizens were called before Congress and personally ruined for exercising their constitutional right to remain silent. Some were imprisoned. Those who refused to take "loyalty oaths" could be fired from jobs or face social ostracism. Simple advocacy of communism as the best form of government was seen by many as a reason for arrest. The McCarthy hysteria, as with the Japanese internment, also played to existing ethnic prejudices, as many of the victims of McCarthyism were Jewish Americans.

would follow. The Justice Department, led by Attorney General John Ashcroft, was determined that all measures necessary to prevent a similar attack be taken.

Since the attackers had all been noncitizens, one of Ashcroft's first moves was to increase the period of time that immigrants could be held without charges. Very quickly, hundreds were arrested, often without knowing why the FBI had appeared at their homes or places of work, guns drawn. The right of the arrested to at least know the charges against them is one of the most fundamental limits on police and investigators. It forms the core of all rights of the accused. How can one contest the legality of one's imprisonment without knowing the precise nature of the charges? Months later, several detainees alleged that the government denied them access to attorneys.

Ashcroft also issued an order that in certain cases the right of attorney–client privilege would not be honored by the Justice Department. This right has been seen as vital to the preservation of the adversarial criminal justice system, as without it an accused person may not confide in his or her attorney and receive the best legal advice. Facing mounting criticism for his unilateral action on attorney–client privilege, Ashcroft retreated somewhat by noting that only 16 of the 158,000 federal prisoners were having communications with their attorneys monitored. Ashcroft's unprecedented move was motivated by the fear that terrorists might use friendly or naive attorneys to pass instructions to confederates about future terrorist acts. He promised that no evidence obtained through the monitoring would be used in criminal trials but only to ensure public safety.

The government also refused to name those it had in custody or even to give the number of those arrested. Ashcroft first defended not releasing a list of the detainees by saying he did not want to expose those arrested to the embarrassment of public revelation. Given the public mood against terrorists, the government argued that they were actually protecting the accused and their families from public reaction against them. When many families and lawyers of the detainees rejected this argument, Ashcroft shifted tactics. He argued instead that releasing a list would play into the hands of al-Qaeda by telling them which members of their terrorist network were captured and which were still available to carry out actions against the United States.

The controversy over the detainees grew as stories of abuse appeared in the media. One case that received widespread attention was that of Mohammed Irshaid, a Jordanian who had lived in America for 22 years. Irshaid, a civil engineer, was arrested at work, handcuffed in front of his colleagues, and taken to jail in New Jersey on alleged violation of immigration regulations. Not only was the arrest "the most humiliating thing to happen to me in my life," but Irshaid's Islamic faith was also mocked by guards. After three weeks of captivity, Irshaid was released; no charges were ever filed. Osama Awadallah, another Jordanian with permanent residency status, was jailed for three months and kicked and beaten during his imprisonment. (Awadallah later became the first detainee to sue the government over his treatment.) The government refused to tell some of the families where their loved ones were being held and delayed all communication. Many families feared for their relative's safety, with ample justification. Hasnain Javed, a Pakistani national living with his aunt in Houston, was pulled off a bus in Alabama and arrested by the Border Patrol for a visa violation. After being placed in a county jail in Mississippi, Javed was beaten for 20 minutes by other inmates while guards watched. As the inmates called Javed "bin Laden," they stripped him of his clothing, fractured his ribs, ruptured his eardrum, and broke one of his teeth. People with only the most peripheral connection to the attacks, or with none at all, were held without charges. Some were held as "material witnesses," and even the government did not allege they were guilty of any wrongdoing. Although it is difficult to know for sure, civil libertarians estimate that more than 1,200 persons were detained at some point in the post–September 11 security arrests.

The American public was untroubled by the actions of the attorney general and indeed gave broad support for the aggressive acts against immigrants. A *Newsweek* poll found that 86 percent of the public felt the government's actions were appropriate, and few political figures spoke out against the arrests or the lack of information from the Justice Department. One exception was Senator Russ Feingold (D-Wis.), who had a long record on questions of civil liberties. Feingold publicized the Justice Department's treatment of Awadallah and other detainees. He also responded angrily to the suggestion made by Attorney General Ashcroft and others that such criticism was aiding bin Laden: "Members of Congress and public interest organizations have been told that our effort to oversee the Justice Department's investigation is tantamount to aiding the terrorists. That accusation is not only untrue, it is offensive in a democracy." Still, despite criticism from civil libertarians and some members of Congress, six months after September 11, detainees still languished in prison, not charged with any crime and pleading that they had no connection to the attacks on America.

In addition to the nationwide arrests, the Justice Department asked for and received the cooperation of local police authorities in interviewing 5,000 Middle Eastern men who shared certain demographic traits with the September 11 terrorists. The "Responsible Cooperators Program" offered fast-track naturalization and the possibility of U.S. citizenship even for illegal immigrants who provided especially helpful information. The interviews were entered into a new computer database designed to help the government prevent future terrorist attacks. Although the effort was voluntary, some criticized it as "racial profiling." Assistant Attorney General Michael Chertoff defended the program in testimony before Congress: "This is the least intrusive type of investigative technique one can imagine . . . this is approaching people and asking them if they will respond to questions." However, critics worried that it resembled the massive surveillance of suspected communists practiced by the government from the 1930s through the 1970s. Using local police forces as well as federal agents, the government amassed hundreds of thousands of files on innocent U.S. citizens. But preeminent political scientist James Q. Wilson argued that these fears were groundless. "Whatever happens today will happen in a very different environment. The country has responded . . . in a sober and adult way." Wilson and others were confident that the government would not repeat historic abuses of civil rights common in earlier crises.

The next step for the Justice Department may be to apprehend, question, and deport the estimated 6,000 illegal immigrants of Middle Eastern descent who have already ignored prior deportation orders. Is it racial profiling for the government to focus on these immigrants among the more than 314,000 violators of deportation orders? Given that no illegal immigrant has the right to be in the country, particularly following a deportation hearing, it is unlikely that concerns about the selective deportation of certain ethnic groups will slow the next phase of the government's post–September 11 security plan.

THE USA PATRIOT ACT: CONGRESS GIVES ASHCROFT ITS APPROVAL

The Justice Department also sought new legislative powers to conduct the war against terrorism. Polls showed that the public was strongly in favor of the legislation, and most members of Congress were supportive. As after the 1995 Oklahoma City bombing, Congress seemed willing to listen to prosecutors and investigators who wanted to "plug holes" in America's domestic security. The administration's proposal was titled the USA PATRIOT Act, an unwieldy acronym for Uniting and Strengthening America by Providing Appropriate Tools Required to Intercept and Obstruct Terrorism. Despite the use of such a soothing title, there were those who worried that the administration's legislation went too far. Senate Judiciary committee chairman Patrick Leahy (D-Vt.) cautioned that "if we shred the Constitution, the terrorists win." Criticism also came from the right. Representative Bob Barr (R-Ga.), one of the most conservative members of Congress, stated, "We cannot and must not allow our constitutional freedoms to become victim of these violent attacks."

What new powers had the government sought? First, an expanded ability to wiretap phones. Previously, wiretaps could occur only after a search warrant had been issued by a magistrate, specifying the phone that was to be tapped. The Justice Department argued that in the age of cellular phones, this was a great impediment to anti-terrorism efforts. A terrorist group could simply buy new cell phones every month and prevent effective monitoring of their planning. Investigators sought to have roving wiretapping warrants that allow tapping of any phone in a suspect's personal use. Wiretapping warrants under the Foreign Intelligence and Surveillance Act (FISA) would also last longer and have broader effect. In addition, the FBI sought to expand its surveillance of e-mail and computers, potentially allowing it to sift through millions of e-mails and Web sites searching for suspicious words and phrases. The legislation provided for enhanced use of the Regional Information Sharing System, which allowed local and state police to easily gain data on terrorists. In addition, the power to detain and speedily deport foreigners was sought, as was the power to more efficiently investigate international money laundering, one of the key conduits of support for terrorism. Nadine Strossen, the president of the American Civil Liberties Union, the most prominent interest group safeguarding the rights of individuals, joined others in fiercely opposing aspects of Ashcroft's proposal. "All of these provisions together will amount to a breathtaking expansion of federal power."

Ashcroft's opening statement to Congress in defense of the new powers was tactically brilliant. Knowing that he would face criticism primarily from Democrats, he chose to compare himself to a liberal icon, Bobby Kennedy. Kennedy, as attorney general in the early 1960s, had encouraged aggressive tactics against organized crime, and Ashcroft argued that similar tough and innovative uses of the law and the police were justified by September 11. The debate over civil liberties was sharp and painful. While Ashcroft called on all Americans to aid in the effort, he also criticized those who would question the new measures as abettors of terrorism, a stance that angered some liberal senators.

In the end, though, Congress adjusted some aspects of Ashcroft's request, and the legislation passed 98 to 1 in the Senate and with fewer than 60 opposition votes in the House. The most important adjustment that Congress requested in the bill was the addition of a "sunset" provision. If the law were not reauthorized by Congress in four years, it would become inactive. Many, such as liberal senator Paul Wellstone (D-Minn.), saw the addition of a sunset provision as vital. This way, if

Attorney General John Ashcroft aggressively sought new powers for the federal government in the war on terror at home. As head of the Justice Department, Ashcroft was central in several key decisions, including the USA PATRIOT Act, the move for military tribunals, and the treatment of American Taliban John Walker Lindh.

the powers granted were abused, Congress would have an easier mechanism by which to check the administration than the passing of new legislation.

The passage of the USA PATRIOT Act was a forgone conclusion in the aftermath of September 11. The threat to civil liberties from future government abuse of the new powers was hypothetical and abstract for most Americans and most members of Congress. The threat of new terrorist acts by contrast seemed real and immediate.

MILITARY TRIBUNALS AND POWS:
RIGHTS FOR TERRORISTS?

Should those who would destroy the Bill of Rights enjoy its protection?

MILTON CUMMINGS AND DAVID WISE, POLITICAL ANALYSTS

As the Bush administration contemplated a war against terror in Afghanistan and elsewhere, the question immediately arose: What should happen to any terrorists apprehended alive? Should they be brought to the United States and tried by the federal judiciary? Should an international tribunal be established, using the mechanism of the World Court or the United Nations? Or should a military tribunal be established, following a precedent set during World War II?

The Bush administration issued an executive order on November 13 setting up military tribunals for suspected terrorists. These tribunals would be presided over by military officers, in secret if necessary, and normal rules of evidence would not apply. Hearsay and illegally obtained evidence, for example, could be admit-

What Is the FISA Court?

The Foreign Intelligence and Surveillance Act (FISA), passed in 1978, was designed to bring judicial scrutiny to the domestic actions of the National Security Agency (a top-secret intelligence agency tasked with monitoring, decoding, and analyzing international communications, among other duties), the CIA, and the FBI. Congressional investigations had revealed widespread wiretapping of domestic political opponents of the president, such as actress Jane Fonda and civil rights leader Martin Luther King Jr. Under the leadership of FBI Director J. Edgar Hoover, many domestic political groups were harassed and unlawfully infiltrated by the FBI, usually with no warrant or judicial scrutiny. Under FISA, domestic surveillance requires a warrant, issued by a member of a panel of federal judges, appointed by the chief justice of the Supreme Court. The FISA court judges, who serve seven-year terms, come to Washington for two-week rotations to oversee requests for wiretapping and break-ins by the FBI and other agencies in defense of American interests at home. For example, if the FBI suspects that a federal employee is spying for a foreign power, they may break in to the suspect's home, plant listening devices, and monitor every aspect of the suspect's life. A FISA warrant differs from a criminal warrant for wiretapping. In a criminal warrant, the police are required to show probable cause of criminal activity to a magistrate. In a FISA warrant, the government need only establish that the suspect is an agent of a foreign power. This lighter burden of proof had an effect: from 1996 to 2000, of the 4,275 requests for wiretaps or break-ins, all 4,275 were approved.

The USA PATRIOT Act expanded the use of FISA warrants by granting roving wiretapping powers to federal agencies and by lengthening the period of the initial warrant from 45 days to 120 days, with the possibility of extension to one year with a judge's approval. The act also added four new judges to the FISA court in anticipation of greater surveillance.

Are civil libertarians correct to worry about the abuse of FISA powers? In some ways, the FISA court remains a check on the executive's ability to use domestic surveillance for malignant purposes.

In the past, the FBI or the Justice Department needed no one's approval to wiretap and break in to the homes of American citizens in the name of national security. While the judges of the court almost never turn down a request, they ask for clarifications and changes in the scope of some of the warrants before they issue approval. In addition, the Justice Department may not bring many "gray area" requests before the court. The Justice Department decided not to present a FISA request to the court in the case of Zacarias Moussaoui, the alleged 20th hijacker, prior to September 11 because they did not feel they had evidence that would pass the court's scrutiny. But what concerns civil libertarians perhaps most of all is the secrecy under which the court and the resulting wiretapping and break-ins operate. If an American rents a room to a foreign student who has come under suspicion and shares a phone or computer with him or her, months of the American's private conversations and e-mails may now be cataloged by the federal government's police agencies without consent or even notification. Even conversations and intimate moments between residents in the house may be monitored through bugs planted following a break-in. Remember, too, that the standards for issuing a FISA warrant are lower than for a criminal warrant.

It is impossible to know how many of the thousands of FISA warrants were granted against persons entirely innocent of espionage or terrorism or how many untargeted people also lost their privacy. What can be known to a near certainty is that the number of times that the privacy of Americans will be encroached on in the name of national security will rise in the aftermath of September 11. Whether you approve of such acts is a function of how much you value privacy and how much you fear the terrorist threat. It also depends on how much you trust your government. For many Americans, the fact that the existing standards for a FISA warrant prevented the investigation of Moussaoui's computer indicates that our government has put too high a value on privacy at the cost of our safety.

ted. Nor would unanimity or proof beyond a reasonable doubt be necessary for a guilty verdict. Defendants would not have the right to challenge the verdict before the federal judiciary, nor would they necessarily have the right to an attorney of their choosing. These proposals were widely criticized at home and abroad for their limitations on the civil rights of the accused. An editorial in the *New York Times* labeled the military tribunals "a travesty of justice . . . a dangerous idea, made even worse by the fact that it is so superficially attractive."

Why did the Bush administration choose this method? Administration officials made it clear that the other options were unworkable or highly undesirable. Although supporters of domestic trials pointed to the successful prosecution of the terrorists who attacked the World Trade Center in 1993 and America's African embassies in 1998, supporters of military tribunals noted that domestic trials had damaged America's security. In the public trial of al-Qaeda members in 2000, it had become obvious that America's intelligence agencies were monitoring the use of satellite telephones by bin Laden and terrorist leaders. As soon as this knowledge got out, al-Qaeda stopped using the phones. Thus, public trials had made terrorism harder to detect and harder to prevent. Military tribunals would protect sources and methods of U.S. intelligence. Other supporters of tribunals worried that terror cases could clog the federal judiciary and become media circuses.

Some critics, particularly on the left, argued that the appropriate response to the attacks of September 11 was an international tribunal to try suspected terrorists. This would build the moral legitimacy of America in the eyes of the world and fight the growing impression of the nation as a unilateral cowboy making its own rules. However, as Ruth Wedgwood, a professor of international law at Yale University pointed out, international justice could be agonizingly slow. The tribunal set up to punish those who violated human rights in the former Yugoslavia had already taken eight years and more than $400 million to try 31 defendants. Would this deter terrorism or provide timely information on the structure of the international terrorist network to aid in the prevention of future terrorist acts?

These arguments convinced most Americans that military tribunals of some kind were the best way to try terrorist suspects, at least foreign nationals captured abroad. However, the question of the exact legal status of the captured quickly became an issue as the war against the Taliban rapidly resulted in hundreds of detainees. Were these men "prisoners of war" under the international law known as the Geneva Convention? The Bush administration's first response was an emphatic *no*. Under their interpretation of the convention, terrorists were not covered, as they fought without identifying themselves with uniforms and targeted civilians rather than military facilities. While the Bush administration promised to treat them with appropriate measures, they refused to label them prisoners of war. The decision was again influenced by the need to prosecute further the war on terror. Under the Geneva Convention, prisoners must generally be released as soon as hostilities end. Moreover, they are not required to give any more information than their names and their military ranks.

The POW issue bedeviled the Bush administration for months. International criticism was sharp. Because America was going to try terrorists in military tribunals without any guidance under international law, some of the nation's clos-

Roosevelt's Use of Military Tribunals: Cautionary Tale or Applicable Precedent?

When the Bush administration announced its decision to create military courts to try terrorists, it relied on the precedent of the trials of eight Nazi saboteurs in 1942. Shortly after America entered World War II, two teams of German agents were secretly dropped off on American shores by submarines. One of the spies alerted the FBI to the danger before any sabotage was carried out. Thus, the only crime with which the Nazis could have been charged was attempted sabotage, a minor felony. In addition, much of the evidence would not have been admissible in a civilian trial. Roosevelt opted to create a military tribunal, with severely limited rights of appeal and other constrictions on normal court behavior. Within seven weeks, six of the defendants were electrocuted. Despite a promise from the FBI for leniency, the spy who brought the plot to the attention of the authorities was sentenced to 40 years. The Supreme Court, under extreme pressure from the executive, approved of the executions immediately without issuing an opinion. In any case, Roosevelt had stated to his attorney general that he would under no circumstances allow the men to escape conviction.

As historians have studied the case in recent years, troubling aspects continue to emerge. While the Supreme Court did approve the executions, when they later tried to write an opinion justifying the decision, they found it difficult to square what had been done with earlier Supreme Court precedents. Even justices who had enthusiastically endorsed the execution of the saboteurs now regretted the decision, one labeling the trials "not a happy precedent." The secrecy in which those trials were conducted has also been questioned. Yale University law professor Neil Katyal told Congress in November 2001, "The real reason President Roosevelt authorized these military tribunals was to keep evidence of the FBI's bungling of the case secret." After the trial, the secrecy continued as the government guarded many of the facts of the trial to protect the reputation of Hoover and others. Katyal and others also pointed out that the case of the Nazi saboteurs was inapplicable to the current situation because it had been upheld by the Supreme Court only because of the congressional declaration of war in 1941, which has not occurred in the present war on terrorism.

However, despite these objections, the Bush administration continued to refer in statements to the example set by Roosevelt. In invoking Roosevelt and World War II, the Bush administration evoked a popular war and a popular wartime president.

est allies refused to hand over al-Qaeda members that they had arrested in post–September 11 crackdowns. European countries in particular seemed reluctant to cooperate with the Bush administration's style of justice, in part because of continuing disagreements over the death penalty, which is banned in every western European nation. The military tribunals and POW issues also were embarrassing to some American interest groups that had been working for international human rights. How could the United States, which had a long record of criticizing the use of military tribunals by Third World countries, adopt them? How could the United States ask nations such as China to uphold international law when it was widely seen by the world as noncompliant with the Geneva Convention, perhaps the most well known component of international law?

Cracks within the Bush administration also emerged as some in the State Department and the Defense Department questioned the wisdom of the POW policy. Some U.S. military leaders worried that the POW decision might one day come back to haunt U.S. troops. It became clear during the conflict in Afghani-

The American Taliban: Civil Liberties and John Walker Lindh

The American media made much of the capture by U.S. forces of John Walker Lindh, a 20-year-old American who had joined the Taliban months before the September 11 attacks. Not only had he allegedly been trained at an al-Qaeda camp, but he had also battled U.S. and Northern Alliance forces during the war against Afghanistan. Moreover, in an interview with the U.S. media after his capture, he voiced support for the attacks on the World Trade Center.

Lindh presented Bush with a tough decision: How should he be treated? Should he be tried abroad by a military tribunal? If he should get different treatment from other al-Qaeda members, at what point did the military need to turn him over to civilian authorities? Did he immediately possess all the rights that an American citizen would have following an arrest? For example, should he be interrogated by the military without access to a lawyer? If so, was his testimony admissible in a U.S. court?

Ultimately, the Justice Department decided that Lindh would be tried in America in a civilian trial in federal court. Lindh was charged with conspiracy to kill U.S. nationals and providing material support and resources to foreign organizations, among other crimes. If convicted, Lindh faces three life terms plus another 90 years in prison. His lawyers intend to contest that much of the evidence against their client was produced in violation of his civil rights and should therefore be thrown out of court. Another difficult issue facing the judge in his case is whether an unbiased jury can be found to hear objectively the charges against a young man who supported the slaughter of Americans in New York and Washington.

stan that hundreds if not thousands of U.S. troops were taking part in warfare while camouflaged as Afghanis. If U.S. special forces were to be captured while taking part in a future military engagement, would they be denied POW status and subjected to mistreatment using the precedent set by the Bush administration? The Bush administration adjusted its position one more time in the face of the mounting criticism, now saying that the detainees (flown to a U.S. base in Cuba) were being treated with all the privileges of POW status while not being recognized as such. This change did not end criticism abroad. Still, Vice President Cheney and other administration officials were adamant that military trials without POW status was the correct way to proceed.

Many foreign countries remained unconvinced by this logic, pointing out that it left the detainees in legal limbo, eligible for status neither as foreign nationals charged with criminal acts nor as POWs under the Geneva Convention. In February 2002, two British citizens and one Australian detainee sued in federal court, alleging that their constitutional right to due process had been violated.

The domestic criticism was more procedural, perhaps because most Americans believed that whatever treatment was accorded members of al-Qaeda could not be harsh enough. What bothered some constitutional scholars was the manner in which Bush had decided to use military tribunals and to avoid granting POW status. Under the Constitution, the power to establish all courts is absolutely granted to Congress. While Roosevelt's 1942 order establishing a military tribunal for Nazi saboteurs was upheld by the Supreme Court, the Court relied on Congress' declaration of war against Germany and Japan to support its opinion. In ad-

A Time for Torture? Reconsidering the Fifth Amendment

Among the most precious civil liberties that the accused have enjoyed in America is the right against self-incrimination, enshrined in the Fifth Amendment. This right grew directly out of the use of torture by authorities in Great Britain for centuries. Although rogue police officers in America have used torture, particularly against racial minorities, the practice has never been accepted as constitutional. After 9-11, legal scholars asked whether the government should be permitted to use torture if it could prevent, for example, the explosion of a nuclear weapon in a downtown urban center. The widespread death and destruction of September 11, carried out by a conspiracy of terrorists, brought this law school hypothetical to reality for some Americans. One of the nation's leading liberal constitutional experts, Harvard University's Alan Dershowitz, even advocated a "torture warrant" in which a judge would consider the government's need for torture on a case-by-case basis. Dershowitz, while not advocating torture, felt that if it was going to happen, it needed judicial oversight.

Other nations still use torture. In fact, the American government has in the past knowingly deported suspects to allied nations, hoping that their police forces would be able to extract through torture information that American authorities could not legally obtain. The mere threat of deportation to a nation such as Jordan or Egypt has proved to be effective in getting information from American detainees. In the aftermath of September 11, some wondered whether the threat to America now justified the domestic use of torture. Some pointed out that Israel, the nation with the greatest experience in dealing with terrorism, has used "moderate physical pressure," or mild torture, for years. Although the Israeli government claims that it uses torture only to gain information that could immediately save innocent lives, human rights groups have complained that torture is widely used to punish Palestinian militants.

Currently, no political figure has advocated the use of torture in America, but the mere appearance of the idea of torture in the popular press demonstrates how September 11 changed the way Americans think about civil liberties. Should more terrorist attacks occur, perhaps even this most cherished limit on government power could fall.

dition, in regard to the POWs, the Constitution gives the power to set rules of capture to Congress. Not only did the White House decide both issues by executive order, but it barely consulted Congress on how it should proceed.

It is difficult to know why the Bush administration did not ask Congress to pass a bill authorizing military tribunals or consult with Congress on the status of the detainees. There would have been little opposition from Congress or the public to almost every measure the administration desired. It may, however, have been precisely the knowledge that there would be little domestic opposition that allowed Bush to proceed unilaterally. In early February, the American Bar Association, the largest professional organization representing America's attorneys, voted to ask Bush to conduct terrorism trials in accordance with the standards practiced for U.S. court-martial proceedings. Suspects would have right to appeal to the Supreme Court, and unanimity would be required in death sentencing. The Pentagon has not yet announced what rules would ultimately govern any military tribunals, but it seems possible that some of the criticism of Bush's original plans may result in compromises that will enhance the rights of suspected terrorists.

THE FUTURE OF CIVIL LIBERTIES
IN THE ONGOING CRISIS

Whenever civil liberties are discussed, opponents of new government limits on individual rights speak of a "slippery slope." They worry that even if new measures can be justified by current threats to national security, these measures may serve as precedents for ominous future encroachments on personal freedoms. Wiretapping that is strictly limited to agents of foreign powers may be expanded to include opposition-party figures, as occurred in other countries and even in this country. Information that the government today gathers for benign purposes may be used by some future government for tyrannical purposes. Once the government starts down a slippery slope, there may be no way to stop the loss of further liberties. For example, the National Rifle Association and other defenders of the rights of gun owners have opposed efforts to license gun owners and register handguns because they fear that such legislation would only be the first step toward gun bans and confiscation.

The attacks of September 11 caused many ideas that had been rejected because of such fears to be considered anew. One example is a national identity card. Such a card could be required either for all residents or only for immigrants and noncitizens. Unlike many nations, the United States has no universally recognized national identity card. Passports in America are typically used only for international travel, and driver's licenses are issued by the states and are subject to state regulations. Compared to the proposed national identity card, driver's licenses are easily forged and fraudulently obtained. Indeed, several of the terrorists of September 11 had driver's licenses. Potentially, Americans could be required to carry the national identity card and present it when making major purchases, traveling on airplanes, conducting public business, or entering federal buildings. Identity cards could be encoded with the distinctive record of a physical feature, such the holder's fingerprints, making them difficult or impossible to forge. This would be very helpful to law enforcement at all levels of American society in the fight against crimes such as credit card theft, fraud, drug trafficking, and income tax evasion. A national identity card would also make it much more difficult for terrorists, as well as other criminals, to hide in the anonymity of American cities and towns.

The government has considered mandating national identity cards in the past to fight such problems as illegal immigration, but these proposals had always been defeated, in part by the slippery-slope concerns of civil libertarians. A national identity card might well put too much information in the hands of government. Today, a warrant is often required before various government agencies can share information about citizens. For example, the Internal Revenue Service and the Social Security Administration do not make their files on income immediately open to other federal agencies. Civil libertarians worried that a national identity card would be the first step in the creation of a universal data bank containing every aspect of citizens' personal lives. While they concede that it would make law enforcement far more efficient, they worry about the loss of freedom and privacy that would, they believe, inevitably result. The history of data banks held by federal and state authorities offers little comfort to those who worry about privacy and the abuse of such information.

The national identity card has not yet received the support of the Bush administration or any major figures in Congress. It remains on the horizon, along with other civil liberties questions. The attacks of September 11 even raised the issue of the role the military will play in America's domestic security. Since 1878, the Posse Comitatus Act has prevented active-duty military personnel from making domestic arrests or conducting searches on American citizens. At the time of the attacks, the U.S. military had no specific command tasked with defending the borders of the United States except the air defense system designed to monitor Cold War–era bomber and missile attacks. The military now proposes the creation of a new military command encompassing the United States (and possibly Canada and Mexico), raising the specter of domestic use of the massive power of the Pentagon. These fears appear fantastical and overblown to many Americans. Yet few would have imagined how rapidly and radically our civil liberties could change before September 11. If another large-scale terrorist attack occurs, the government's power could grow yet again.

Perhaps contractions in civil liberties after September 11 were only natural. Terrorism may be thought of as a disease attacking the body politic, necessitating the ingestion of strong medicine, such as the measures strengthening the power of government to wiretap or to hold detainees without charges. Once the body politic is rid of the disease of terrorism, these measures should be repealed. Yet watchdogs of America's civil liberties, on both the right and the left of the political spectrum, fear that these liberties, once given up, will not easily be reclaimed by citizens. No less an authority than Attorney General Ashcroft promised that the new era of government surveillance would last for many years. Those who attacked America on September 11 cynically exploited America's open society, its liberties, and its technological prowess to make a sick and twisted protest against the policies of this country. Among the casualties of their evil acts was the breadth of freedom and privacy that Americans had enjoyed as a birthright. Long after the hole in the Pentagon is repaired and Ground Zero in lower Manhattan rebuilt, the damage that the terrorists did to American liberties may well linger.

4

※

Public Opinion in Crisis: Rally 'Round Whose Flag?

The New York Rangers and the Philadelphia Flyers were playing an intense game of hockey at the First Union Center in Philadelphia on September 20, 2001. At the end of the second period, the score was tied, 2 to 2. During the break, the management of the arena decided to put the live feed of President Bush's speech to Congress on the Jumbotron screen. When the break ended, the players returned to the ice, and the broadcast ceased. A chant arose from the crowd: "Leave it on! Leave it on!" The game was halted, the speech reappeared on the screen, and the crowd at the First Union Center watched as Bush described his plans for leading the nation in the fight against terror. When the speech was over, a tie game was declared, and the crowd cheered. If even the rabid sports fans of Philadelphia felt that a speech by the president was more important than their beloved Flyers defeating the hated Rangers, clearly politics had returned, however briefly, to the center of American life.

The number of Americans willing to watch a speech by a president had been dropping for decades. Particularly since the advent of cable television, the audience for presidential addresses and debates had been shrinking. Now, polls conducted by Robert Putnam at Harvard University confirmed that Americans were more interested in politics than they had been even during the protracted battle over the 2000 presidential election results. September 11 changed more than the presidency, Congress, and the institutions of American government; it changed more than the laws of the nation and the nature of our civil liberties. September 11 fundamentally altered the way Americans thought about their government, the man in the White House, the two parties, freedom, and even God and the role of religion in public life. Surely, some of these effects are temporary and indeed are already fading. However, some may have long-lasting effects on American politics. Events such as September 11 can forever shape the political beliefs of a generation. What September 11 means for America is not something that elites alone can determine; in a very real sense, its meaning will be decided by all Americans, one by one, as they work out their own reactions to the horrors inflicted on Washington and New York.

PUBLIC OPINION IN CRISIS IN A THEORETICAL CONTEXT

Few areas of public opinion are as well established as the response of the American citizenry to national crises and military actions. The population rallies around the president specifically and the government generally. Presidential approval goes up, almost regardless of the actions taken by the president. When President Kennedy involved U.S. intelligence and military forces in supporting a disastrous invasion of Cuba by Cuban exiles in 1961, his approval ratings went up. This occurred even though the invasion was a monumental failure and an international embarrassment. Similarly, when American hostages were taken by the government of Iran in 1979, President Carter's approval ratings went up, even though he did little to respond or improve the situation. Americans almost instinctively react to international threats by rallying in support of national institutions and figures.

What is less well established is how long such effects will last. Again, the example of President Carter is instructive. While the nation rallied to him in the early weeks and months of the crisis, disenchantment with him rose steadily as the Carter policy failed to bring the hostages home. The American public wants to see that the president is responding to a crisis with steadfast determination and effective leadership. The patience of the public is not limitless. It was vital to the success of President Roosevelt's wartime public approval that America finally started to win a few battles after a long series of losses to Japan starting at Pearl Harbor. Lincoln's leadership of the nation through its darkest hours during the Civil War was a tenuous matter, as he lost the support of much of the Northern public before the victories of General Grant restored the nation's confidence in the president. Clearly, the length of the "rally effect" has something to do with meeting the public's expectations, but exactly how this is done and how it can be measured in new crises is difficult to grasp.

American public opinion may be subject to particular volatility in crises that involve foreign policy. Political scientist Gabriel Almond has found that on foreign affairs, as opposed to domestic issues, most Americans have "formless and plastic moods" subject to sudden shifts. The public has little information and few opinions about international relations in normal times. When most citizens are uninformed and unfocused on a topic, experts expect that public opinion can more easily be influenced on that question. Compare the public's opinion on the abortion question to its attitude toward international terrorism prior to September 11. Abortion is a question that most Americans have an opinion about, either because of their religious backgrounds or because of family values. It is a topic that many families discuss at home and one that comes up almost naturally among friends and lovers. It would be very difficult for a president or other political figure to rapidly change American public opinion on abortion. By contrast, the public knew almost nothing about terrorism on September 11 and was desperate to learn more about it. Most citizens had not thought deeply about terrorism; rare indeed were the American homes in which the correct policy toward international terrorism came up prior to September 11. In a 1998 Harris poll, only 4 percent of Americans identified terrorism as an important issue, behind dozens of other concerns. In 1996, the Pew Research Center concluded bluntly that "the public is not particularly concerned about any kind of terrorism in the United States." The sudden appearance of terrorism as the foremost concern of most Americans may allow political elites, particularly the president, to have a tremendous influence on framing the issue of terrorism and affecting what conclusions Americans come to about this new and frightening issue in American politics.

Another aspect of public opinion in crisis that is less well understood is why certain national crises have lingering partisan effects and others seem to have no influence on how Americans think about the two parties. Roosevelt's bold leadership through the Great Depression and World War II had lasting effects on the two-party system, creating the "New Deal Coalition" that dominated American politics at least until 1968. From 1933 on, the Democratic Party was the majority party in America, reliably winning congressional majorities in both houses and taking the presidency four of the next five elections. Roosevelt's leadership in crisis led to an electoral realignment in which one party took the majority status from the other. The polar opposite of such a lasting effect was seen with George H. W. Bush in 1990–1991 during the Persian Gulf War. Bush successfully led the nation through its largest foreign military engagement since Vietnam. The nation rallied to Bush in the crisis and rewarded him with sky-high approval ratings when U.S. forces won a quick victory over Iraq. However, Bush's popularity faded quickly, and his party reaped no benefits at all. Eighteen months after Bush rode as high as any president had in the polls, he went down to a crushing personal defeat, and the Democrats took control of the White House and Congress for the first time since 1980.

Part of the explanation for why some crises have partisan implications may lie in the "imprinting" effect of a crisis on the political socialization of a generation. Sociologist Karl Mannheim argued in the early 20th century that young people may be deeply affected by the mood of the nation when they enter the political world for the first time. This is particularly true in times of great clashes and crises, such as wars and economic depressions. Mannheim argued that a generation can be imprinted by such events and remain forever different from other generations who were older or not alive during that crisis. This imprinting model does seem to explain the lasting influence of the Great Depression and World War II. Those Americans who were between the ages of 14 and 24 during that period were far more Democratic than other Americans throughout their lives. Consider what they learned about politics when they were at their most impressionable: Roosevelt and the Democratic Party saved America from economic destruction and then saved the world from fascism. While the truth of these assertions is very much open to question, they were widely believed at the time. By contrast, the Persian Gulf War was too short and too distant to affect the political socialization of young people. There was no widespread agreement about the larger meaning of the war and whether either party should be rewarded with enhanced loyalty. One of the most important questions yet to be answered about September 11 is whether it will have lasting partisan implications for Republicans and Democrats. The key may well be the interpretation that America's young people give to the events of September 11 and the government's response.

THE PREDICTABLE RALLY: BUSH, FORCE, AND COUNTRY RIDE HIGH IN THE POLLS

The immediate reaction to September 11 among the U.S. public was to strongly support the president, the military, and the government. Many Americans had harbored doubts about Bush's qualifications to be president, and some had questioned his legitimacy because of the way the controversial election of 2000 ended. The collapse of the World Trade Center towers seemed to put an end to doubts and questions about Bush. His approval ratings, solid but not impressive prior to September 11, immediately rose to the high 80s and low 90s, almost unprecedented in polling history. What was indeed unprecedented was the longevity of Bush's support; even as late as February, it had scarcely dropped. While data are not as reliably available for pre-1948 periods, and it is possible that Roosevelt's ratings during the war or the Depression may have been equally high at times, it is doubtful that even Roosevelt rode as high in the polls for as long as Bush did. Crucial to Bush's continued dominance of the polls were his speech to Congress on September 20 and his successful leadership of the conflict in Afghanistan.

Of course, an eternal and often unanswerable question in public opinion is how much the mood of Americans is affected by the behavior of elites and how much elite behavior merely reflects the opinions of the country. Did Bush rise in the polls in part because no Democratic leaders were questioning his abilities or his policies? It was difficult to find any critics of the Bush administration in politics or in the media in the days following the attacks on America. Was the public sheepishly following these elite cues to rally to Bush, or, alternatively, were the media and the Democratic leadership supporting Bush because they believed that was what the public demanded? Or were political elites and the public simultaneously coming to the same conclusions independent of each other? It is quite possible that all three explanations have elements of truth to them, illustrating the frustrating complexity of public opinion in a democracy.

One clear message that the American public was sending to its political leaders was that there was strong support for vengeance against those responsible. This response was immediate and probably uninfluenced by any elite framing of the issue. An ABC News/*Washington Post* poll on the evening of September 11 found that 90 percent of Americans advocated the use of the military. Students of American public opinion were not surprised. The American public has long looked

Across the country, and indeed, around the world, Americans gathered to demonstrate their solidarity in the aftermath of 9-11. Few moments in the nation's history had produced such nearly universal outpourings of public sentiment and resolve.

with favor on the use of force in international relations as long as U.S. interests could be shown to be at stake. The "Vietnam syndrome" (see Chapter 1) constrained presidents from deploying U.S. ground forces only in situations where the national interest was unclear. Few Americans felt that there was a lack of clarity about our national interest in responding with strong measures to September 11. By and large, the American public has never ruled out the use of force in international relations, particularly the use of air power or missiles. Indeed, so overwhelming was the response to September 11 that it almost wiped out one of the most reliable findings in public opinion research—that men favor military solutions far more than women do. While men were marginally more bellicose in their attitudes about how hard America should strike back, the overwhelming majority of women agreed.

What was perhaps most significant in the polls following September 11 was the rise in trust in government institutions. Ever since the twin tragedies of Watergate and Vietnam, in which American leaders lied about criminal conduct at home and military actions abroad, the public has had less and less trust in the national government. Polls showed that the experience of September 11 had restored trust in the federal government to a 30-year high. Experts disagree about how long this raised level of trust will continue. Much depends on the success of the war on ter-

---

Beyond the Pale? The Left Wing Comes Under Public Attack After September 11

Although the vast majority of Americans found the attacks of September 11 to be inexplicable acts of evil terrorism, justifying an immediate and overwhelming military response, some voices on the left rose to offer a different view. Of the dissident voices, none attracted more attention than those of writer Susan Sontag and linguist Noam Chomsky. Sontag wrote in the *New Yorker* that much of the commentary by American politicians after September 11 was "self-righteous drivel and outright deceptions."

The voices licensed to follow the event seem to have joined together in a campaign to infantilize the public. Where is the acknowledgment that this was not a "cowardly" attack on "civilization" or "liberty" or "humanity" or "the free world" but an attack on the world's self-proclaimed superpower, undertaken as a consequence of specific American alliances and actions? How many citizens are aware of the ongoing bombing of Iraq? . . . Politics, the politics of a democracy—which entails disagreement, which promotes candor—has been replaced by psychotherapy. Let's by all means grieve together. But let's not be stupid together. . . . "Our country is strong," we are told again and again. I for one don't find that entirely consoling. Who doubts that America is strong? But that's not all America has to be.

Chomsky also called on Americans to examine how U.S. foreign policy played a role in instigating the attacks. While calling them an atrocity, he compared them directly to U.S. bombings on Sudan and other nations. Katha Pollitt, a columnist for the left-wing journal *The Nation,* wrote about her refusal to fly an American flag because it "stands for jingoism and vengeance and war." She worried that war with Afghanistan would reinforce militarism and bigotry in our country and obscure the role that our policy toward Israel and Palestine played in the attacks of September 11. All these viewpoints were widely excoriated by politicians and the media alike.

The American public generally was largely unsympathetic to any attempt to link the acts of the terrorists to U.S. foreign policy. Those on the left who tried to draw that comparison were subjected to intense criticism and scrutiny. However, compared to the blacklisting of communists and socialists during the McCarthy era or the imprisonment or deportation faced by dissidents in World Wars I and II, the treatment of the dissenters of September 11 has been comparatively mild.

---

ror beyond Afghanistan. Still, so far, trust in government, the rise in Bush's approval, and support for the use of force have remained remarkably stable in the months following September 11.

ARABS AND MUSLIMS UNDER ATTACK: THE SEARCH FOR DOMESTIC SCAPEGOATS

The 19 hijackers who killed so many on September 11 were all Arab men of the Islamic faith. Their religion and their nationality were foreign to the vast majority of Americans, and even their strange names and swarthy faces were unusual to many. As in past crises, national unity and rallying behind the government were accompanied by some xenophobia (fear of outsiders) and racial and religious bigotry. Even in educated, highly advanced societies, demagogues arise who exploit crises, and mass hysteria can result. In the 1930s, the leader of Nazi Germany,

Adolf Hitler, staged an attack on the German parliamentary building and blamed it on the Jews. The crisis contributed to the rising tide of anti-Semitism that resulted in the Holocaust. In this country, the shock of Pearl Harbor was followed swiftly by the imprisonment of Japanese Americans in concentration camps (see Chapter 3). Mindful of such dark examples in world history, President Bush made a special effort to remind his countrymen that the perpetrators of the horrors of September 11 were representative neither of Islam nor of the Arab world. Bush visited a mosque, met with Islamic leaders, and asked all Americans to oppose racism and ethnic hatred.

Still, there were isolated acts of violence against Arab Americans and other foreigners. In Mesa, Arizona, Balbir Singh Sodi, the Sikh owner of a Chevron station, was murdered by a deranged gunman. When arrested, the gunman, Frank Roque, claimed to have done the deed because he was "an American" angry about September 11. (Roque's racism was matched only by his ignorance; Sikhs are neither Muslim nor Arab and, as immigrants from India, typically oppose Islamic radicalism.) In Salt Lake City, a Pakistani restaurant was damaged by arson. While it is unknown whether the attack was related to September 11, in response to the widespread belief that it was, local patrons came out the next day to support the family that owned the restaurant, some bearing signs advocating "Peace, Not Hate." In a nation of 260 million, it is tragic but perhaps not surprising that a few Americans responded to September 11 with ignorant acts of xenophobic violence. Following the lead of the president, the overwhelming majority of Americans seemed to be able to separate the hijackers from the Arab or Muslim neighbors living next door.

However, although the public treated Arabs better than the Japanese were treated after Pearl Harbor, the issue of the American public's attitudes toward Arabs and Muslims was not quickly laid to rest. Several citizens of Arab descent were removed from commercial airplanes in the weeks after September 11 because either passengers or crew were made uneasy by their presence. While violent hate crimes were rare, several mosques were vandalized. Some public figures in politics and the media seemed to stoke the fires of anti-Muslim or anti-Arab emotion. Conservative pundit Ann Coulter received international attention for writing that the United States "should invade their [Muslim] countries, kill their leaders and convert them to Christianity." After an uproar, the editors of *National Review,* the leading journal of conservative opinion in the country, fired Coulter. Representative John Cooksey (R–La.) defended racial profiling as simple common sense to a radio reporter, saying, "If I see someone come in that's got a diaper on his head and a fan belt wrapped around the diaper on his head, that guy needs to be pulled over." Cooksey was widely assailed for his statement and apologized. His call for treating those wearing turbans differently was seen to have hurt him in his upcoming race for U.S. Senate.

In February, Christian broadcaster and conservative Republican Pat Robertson said that America's lax immigration policy is "so skewed to the Middle East and away from Europe that we have introduced these people into our midst and undoubtedly there are terrorist cells all over them." Robertson went on to challenge

Beyond the Pale II: The Religious Right Comes Under Attack After 9-11

Two days after September 11, conservative religious broadcaster (and former Republican presidential candidate) Marion "Pat" Robertson invited fellow minister and conservative activist Jerry Falwell to talk on his television show about September 11 and its meaning. During the interview, both men blamed the attacks on liberal groups such as the American Civil Liberties Union (ACLU), gays and lesbians, feminists, and advocates of legalized abortion. Excerpts follow:

Falwell: . . . what we saw on Tuesday, as terrible as it is, could be minuscule if, in fact, God continues to lift the curtain and allow the enemies of America to give us probably what we deserve.

Robertson: Jerry, that's my feeling. I think we've just seen the antechamber to terror. We haven't even begun to see what they can do to the major population.

Falwell: The ACLU's got to take a lot of blame for this.

Robertson: Well, yes.

Falwell: And, I know that I'll hear from them for this. But throwing God out successfully with the help of the federal court system, throwing God out of the public square, out of the schools. The abortionists have got to bear some burden for this because God will not be mocked. And when we destroy 40 million little innocent babies, we make God mad. I really believe that the pagans, and the abortionists, and the feminists, and the gays and the lesbians who are actively trying to make

that an alternative lifestyle, the ACLU, People for the American Way, all of them who have tried to secularize America. I point the finger in their face and say "you helped this happen!"

Robertson: Well, I totally concur, and the problem is we have adopted that agenda at the highest levels of our government. And so we're responsible as a free society for what the top people do. And, the top people, of course, is the court system.

Falwell: Amen.

The criticism of both men was immediate and bitter. Falwell apologized for his remarks, and Robertson initially denied that he had said anything and put the blame entirely on Falwell for the controversy. Most important, the White House made it clear that neither man's comments pleased the president or represented his views. Falwell and Robertson, who had had enormous power in Republican politics at various times, had been abandoned by the leading Republican in the nation.

The American public was largely unwilling to consider whether America was somehow responsible for the attacks of September 11. It did not matter whether it was Jerry Falwell saying America got "probably what we deserve" because of sodomy and abortion or Noam Chomsky finding the root cause in U.S. support for Israel's brutal occupation of Palestinian territories. The question itself was "beyond the pale" following the September 11 attacks.

President Bush's claim that Islam was not evil: "The Koran makes it very clear, if you see an infidel, you are to kill him. . . . They want to coexist until they can control, dominate and then if need be destroy." Ironically, much of Robertson's rhetoric about Islam in America mirrored Taliban rhetoric about Christianity in Afghanistan. Even though Cooksey, Coulter, and Robertson were criticized for their public voicing of religious or ethnic bigotry, they surely reflected an important aspect of the public opinion response to September 11.

Overall, the care with which public expressions of anti-Arab and anti-Muslim expressions were monitored suggests that America has learned from the experiences of past crises.

GOD RETURNS TO PUBLIC LIFE?
SEPTEMBER 11 AND THE EXPRESSION
OF FAITH

Among Western democracies, one of the most distinctive features of American public opinion is the widespread nature of religious faith that appears in polling and focus groups. Compared to citizens of most Western European nations, higher percentages of Americans affirm their belief in God, hold more traditional religious views, and attend religious services more frequently. This has important political ramifications, making issues such as abortion far more contested in American politics. Another much-discussed irony is that while Americans are far more religious than many other advanced countries, the line between church and state is far more zealously policed in this country than in most. Some would argue that it is this line that has preserved the health and vigor of America's religious traditions, while others worry that putting up a wall between church and state will eventually harm America's public institutions. Many Americans experienced September 11 in a deeply personal way, and it is not surprising that many turned to their religious faith to find answers or at least comfort. When, however, U.S. citizens seek to bring their religious faith into the public sphere, there are those who typically oppose this. The months after September 11 exposed this perennial fault line in American politics.

Public opinion polls clearly showed that Americans were looking to God for assistance even in the hours and days immediately following September 11. Polling expert George Gallup averred that at "no other time in recent American history have people turned their faces so readily to God." In Manhattan, some churches reported a doubling in attendance on subsequent Sundays, although the effect did not last. The American Bible Society reported that sales of Bibles rose 42 percent in the months after the attacks. Sales of apocalyptic literature skyrocketed as well, as they tend to do during wars or international crises. The song "God Bless America" was almost as widely heard as the national anthem. There were no objections heard when the members of Congress sang this open plea for the Deity to render his blessings on the nation. However, when it came to the public schools, controversy arose.

The governor of Arkansas sent a letter to school districts in his state urging that they allow students to pray, declaring October "Student Religious Liberty Month." South Carolina's legislature moved toward sponsoring school prayer, and Republicans in the House of Representatives proposed allowing moments of silence for prayer nationwide in the public schools. All these political forces were moved by September 11 to reassert their belief that the Establishment Clause of the Constitution forbids not the public expression of religious faith in public institutions but rather the endorsement of a particular religious faith by the forces of government (this view is known as "accommodationist").

In Mississippi, the Reverend Donald Wildmon found that the attacks of September 11 increased interest in his plan to put the national motto "In God We Trust" in every school in the state and eventually the nation.

Each of these moves by "accommodationist" political forces was resisted by those who see the Constitution as mandating a far stricter separation of church and state. These "separationists" believe that the Establishment Clause commands not just neutrality among religious faiths but that government offer no support to religion generally or exclude those without religious faith in any way, even symbolically. In Rocklin, California, an elementary school that had put "God Bless America" on a marquee in front of the school became the object of national attention. The American Civil Liberties Union demanded that the sign be removed after one parent complained. In response, the House of Representatives passed, by a vote of 404 to 0, a nonbinding "sense of the House" resolution stating that "public schools may display the words 'God Bless America' as an expression of support for the Nation."

The actions by Congress suggested that the tide of public opinion after September 11 was with the accommodationists much more than the separationists. However, the final arbiter of most disputes about separation of church and state is not the court of public opinion but the U.S. Supreme Court. How they will rule on any of these controversies is as yet unknown. What can be known is that the public's turn to religion after the horrors of September 11 reinvigorated a long-running debate about the role of religion in public life.

SEPTEMBER 11 AND GENERATION Y: AWAKENED TO REPUBLICANISM?

If September 11 is going to have a lasting impact on the nature of American public opinion, it will have to be shown to influence the political socialization of the American public, in particular its young people. Political socialization, the process through which a society teaches young people political values and norms, can be greatly influenced by seminal political events such as wars and crises. What imprint will September 11 leave on "Generation Y," also known as "the Millennials"?

What does a seminal political event look like? It must be a crisis or political event that ranks high on the nation's political agenda. It must also be something about which most members of a generation share a common interpretation. The power of the New Deal and World War II in forever shaping the partisan identity of the "Greatest Generation" (Americans born between 1910 and 1930) was that the interpretation of Roosevelt's positive role in both crises was so widely shared. When he passed away, many young Americans could not remember a time when he had not been president (he served from 1933 to 1945, longer than any other chief executive); some described it as equivalent to losing a father. That generation also took a more positive view toward the possibility of government leadership. Even when its members did not become Democrats, the ideological center of American politics shifted, and old-style Republican policies of "laissez-faire" economics became unpopular. Events such as World War II and the Great Depression are obviously rare. While many Americans remember exactly where they were on the day Kennedy was shot, the political message of the assassination of the president was far less obvious. Likewise, although many members of "Generation X" (born between 1961 and 1980) remember where they were when the *Challenger* blew up or when the O.J. Simpson verdict was handed down, the meaning of these events was similarly opaque. The only unifying political events so far shared by the "Millenials" (also known as "Generation Y," born between 1981 and 2000) are the impeachment and trial of President Clinton in 1998–1999 and the prolonged electoral controversy that ended the presidential campaign of 2000. If these events had any universal message, it was arguably that politics was a dirty business.

September 11 and the subsequent war on terrorism could be one of those events that defines a generation and changes the nature of American politics for decades. Political scientist James Gimpel, an expert on the Millennial generation, sees September 11 as "the biggest socializing event of the last 25 or 30 years":

> Until now, this Millennial generation would have had few experiences to direct their political socialization—the Clinton impeachment, the O.J. Simpson trial, maybe—but nothing like Vietnam or Watergate. Until now it seemed like we were seeing the birth of an apolitical or non-political generation . . . this event will awaken these kids to world events and U.S. politics like nothing else in their lifetimes. It will go on and on and on.

Some went so far as to stop calling this "Generation Y" and label it "Generation A," for "Awakened." Behavioral changes were apparent in the months after September 11. Peace Corps applications rose 72 percent in the San Francisco area, and at Smith College the number of students interested in working for the CIA went up exponentially. At Harvard University, students and alumni agitated to return the Reserve Officers' Training Corps (ROTC) to campus, which had been removed from Harvard by the anti-war activism of the baby-boomer generation. While early reports that military enlistments had dramatically increased turned out to be false or exaggerated, there seemed to be an even more positive attitude toward the military in the aftermath of September 11 among the young.

Will September 11 have a partisan effect on the Millennial generation, similar to the New Deal's effect on the Great Depression's generation? Ever since the collapse of the New Deal coalition that dominated American politics from 1933 to 1968, political scientists have expected a partisan "realignment" in which a new majority coalition will emerge. So far, those expectations have not been met, as neither the Democrats nor the Republicans have been able to consistently claim the support of a majority of the population. Polling conducted by a number of firms in early 2002 suggests that the tide of the nation is turning Republican, and this is truer of the young than of the old. While Bush personally benefits from the rally-around-the-flag effect, there is evidence that his party also is gaining support. Karl Rove, Bush's top political adviser, came under fire from Democrats for suggesting that Republicans exploit Bush's wartime popularity directly in the upcoming congressional elections. Rove was only stating the obvious, namely, that the war has produced major public opinion benefits for the Republican Party. Whether those benefits persist through the next election and into the next few decades will be determined in large part by the interpretation that the Millennial generation gives to the war on terrorism. If President Bush successfully leads a multiyear struggle against those who brought down the World Trade Center and their allies, the Millennial generation could become deeply imprinted with a positive attitude toward the Republican Party. Of course, caution is called for when examining shifts in public opinion. Long-term changes in the partisan alignment of the public are typically visible only in retrospect. Anyone who thought that the great Democratic landslide of 1964 or the Republican landslides of 1972 or 1984 represented lasting changes in the American electorate was quickly proven wrong by subsequent events.

Beyond narrow partisan concerns, the deeper meaning of September 11 for the Millennial generation may be that politics matters a great deal and that the world is a dangerous place. These simple lessons could have profound effects on American politics. If politics is seen as important, perhaps participation in elections will rise. If the world is perceived as dangerous, defense spending could continue to rise. Perhaps the most important question yet to be answered is whether September 11 will encourage global involvement in the Millennial generation or whether isolationism (the idea that America should have less to do with other countries, particularly militarily) will begin to characterize the attitudes of America's young people.

5

✳

After the Aftermath: Return to Normalcy or Ongoing Crisis?

On September 11, 2001, the airwaves of the nation were filled with politicians, pundits, and news anchors proclaiming that America would never be the same again—that "everything has changed." What is perhaps most amazing about the response of the American political system to September 11 is that this simply was not true. The resilient patterns of conflict over ideologies, state and federal powers, and interbranch prerogatives have reappeared. Indeed, scant weeks after the attacks, elections were held in Virginia, New Jersey, and New York City itself. Those who expected high turnout as a result of the increased interest in politics following September 11 were disappointed; the turnout was fairly typical—quite low. While low turnout has been criticized as a problem for American democracy, there was something almost comforting about the continuity of alienated apathy or lazy contentment that keeps most Americans away from the voting booth. That, at least, had not been changed by September 11.

However, while it is not true to say that everything has changed, it would be foolish to argue that nothing has been altered by the attacks of September 11. The preceding chapters show that the attacks may have changed the institutions of American government and the contours of American public opinion like no single day since Pearl Harbor or before. The echoes and aftershocks of September 11 will continue to reverberate through our political system for years to come. The question now is, Will American politics ever return to the politics that prevailed on September 10, 2001?

The preceding chapters were about the response of the American domestic political system to an exterior threat: the shocking attack on American civilians and institutions by al-Qaeda. What happens in the next decade within the confines of American domestic politics will be fundamentally influenced by the posture that America takes toward the outside world. Three possible scenarios are briefly outlined here: a return to normalcy, a fortress America, and exponential globalization.

RETURN TO NORMALCY

In this scenario, American politics would look fairly similar to the pre–September 11 status quo. The changes brought about by September 11 would not last or would be largely ignored. The war on terrorism would have no long-term partisan impact, and the status quo of a divided government with no political party achieving majority support in the electorate would continue. Civil liberties, constricted in the months after the attacks, would gradually be won back. America would be unlikely to launch a major assault on Iraq or the other "Axis of Evil" powers, although another Afghanistan-style war could take place in which U.S. troops and air power provide cover for domestic opponents of the current regime. September 11 would not be followed by further terrorist attacks. The powers allocated to the president in the height of the crisis would be gradually returned to Congress and the other power centers in American government without much fanfare or controversy.

FORTRESS AMERICA

If this scenario prevails, American politics would go through a wave of isolationism. The public would want America to be even more heavily armed than it is today to prevent any further attacks. However, the nation would be inclined to follow the lead of populist-conservative Pat Buchanan, who after September 11 argued that "interventionism is the incubator of terrorism." Buchanan and other neoisolationists feel that a fortress America should no longer be so involved with the outside world. Guaranteeing the security of other nations and propping up regimes in Israel, Egypt, and Pakistan fueled the hatred that led to the targeting of American civilians. "Globaloney"—the false beliefs that human rights are universal, democracy should be promoted abroad, and international free trade is an unmitigated good—would also be blamed for the September 11 attacks. This scenario could most plausibly follow if a war against Iraq were prolonged, costly, and unsupported by our major allies in Europe and Asia. It could also follow if further large-scale terrorist attacks take place within America's borders. The balance between civil liberties and order would also remain heavily weighted toward order and away from freedom. Fortress America would be safer but alone and less free. The presidency would be expected to wield more power over the other domestic institutions.

EXPONENTIAL GLOBALIZATION

Rather than seeing in the flames and deaths of September 11 reasons to fear and mistrust the outside world, Americans and their political leaders would gradually embrace the nonterrorist world in the exponential globalization scenario. The

Yards from Ground Zero, in Trinity Church yard in Manhattan, Alexander Hamilton's grave was covered by the debris from the collapsed towers of the World Trade Center.

importance of nation-states, under stress from many complex forces prior to September 11, would continue to decline. America would join other advanced nations in racing toward a future in which citizenship and national boundaries begin to fade. The forces of international trade and international government, represented by the World Trade Organization and the United Nations, would be seen as solutions to the problems that led to September 11. Working with the United Nations and our allies, the United States would involve itself more aggressively in bringing social justice to heavily corrupt and dysfunctional nations, such as Egypt, and would work directly with Israel and the Palestinians to make peace and self-determination a reality in that distressed part of the world. Rather than seeking unilateral military solutions to the problem of Saddam Hussein, multilateral coalitions would be built to address Iraq's pursuit of weapons of mass destruction. Those on the left who see the root causes of suicide bombings in the despair experienced in many parts of the Third World would embrace aspects of exponential globalization, although they would be forced to give up their grave doubts about multinational corporate power. Those on the right who loathe international multilateralism in American foreign policy would be defeated in this scenario. Over the ruins of the World Trade Center, a symbol of globalization in which the remains of citizens of more than 80 nations were interred together, a new world of increasingly globalized values would be built.

HAMILTON'S WARNING, AMERICA'S DECISIONS

Whether America moves toward any of these scenarios in the next decade or toward an entirely different relationship with the outside world will depend on how its leaders and its mass public interpret the events of September 11. It will inevitably depend at least as much on the actions and decisions of men and women in the distant shadows, far beyond the purview of this book and the expertise of its author. Those who conceived, planned, and carried out the cold-blooded mass murders of September 11 sought to instill fear in Americans through the deaths of civilians: terrorism by any definition. As Osama bin Laden said in a post-attack videotape, "This is America, God has sent one of the attacks by God and has attacked one of its best buildings. And this is America, filled with fear from the north, south, east and west, thank God." That fear and the resulting fury were the emotions that wakened the sleeping giant of America—its political system and its public opinion—to authorize the steps outlined in this book: power to the president, deference from Congress, near unanimity in public opinion, war abroad, and limits on liberty at home. Should the new security measures imposed by the government fail and should enemies of Western liberal democracy again perpetrate similar or greater horrors, the consequences for American politics could be unimaginable. The founders of this nation, among the greatest minds to ever wrestle with the questions of governance and freedom, designed a system based on a realistic assessment of human nature. Given the proper education and socialization, humans learn to treasure freedom and guard liberty. But it is innate in human nature for the all-too-human emotion of fear to change the way we feel and think about such questions, as the founders knew.

Alexander Hamilton, along with Madison the greatest advocate of the Constitution, could not have anticipated modern international terrorism, in which four men could kill thousands in an instant. Still, Hamilton well understood what terror could do to a republic. In *The Federalist* No. 8, Hamilton warned that liberty will be the ultimate victim of fear:

> Safety from external danger is the most powerful director of national conduct. Even the ardent love of liberty will, after a time, give way to its dictates. The violent destruction of life and property incident to war, the continual effort and alarm attendant on a state of continual danger, will compel nations the most attached to liberty to resort for repose and security to institutions which have a tendency to destroy their civil and political rights. To be more safe, they at length become willing to run the risk of being less free . . . unavoidably subjected to frequent infringements on their rights, which serve to weaken their sense of those rights . . . by degrees the people are brought to consider the soldiery not only as their protectors, but as their superiors.

Alexander Hamilton, perhaps the greatest New Yorker to ever live, is buried in Trinity Churchyard, scant yards from Ground Zero in Manhattan. The collapse of the World Trade Center towers covered his grave with debris and dust, burying one of freedom's champions beneath terror's momentary triumph. Americans allow the emotion and fear of September 11 to cover Hamilton's prophetic warning about what terror will do to liberty at their grave peril.